UFOs
In The
Bible

Ken Goudsward

ISBN: 978-1-989940-08-2
© 2021 Ken Goudsward
Dimensionfold Publishing

Go and tell this people:
"Be ever hearing, but never understanding;
  be ever seeing, but never perceiving.
Make the heart of this people calloused;
  make their ears dull
  and close their eyes.
Otherwise they might see with their eyes,
  hear with their ears,
  understand with their hearts,
and turn and be healed."
    - Yahweh to the prophet Isaiah

He who has ears to hear, let him hear.
    - Jesus of Nazareth

Table of Contents

Introduction	1
The 1st Kind: Visitations	5
The Three Wise Men	5
Forty Years In The Desert	7
The 2nd Kind: Physical Evidence	9
Scorched Earth	9
Two Camps	10
The 3rd Kind: Beings & Communications	14
Jacob's Ladder	15
Wheels Within Wheels	18
Better Translations	35
A Mighty Wind	37
A Flying Scroll	39
A Fiery Mount	41
A Burning Bush	42
A Missing Ship	44
The Emerald Man	47
The Esteemed	50
The Watchers	52
The Sinai Hikes	53
The Seventy Five	56
The Bard	62
Architecture And Artifacts	67
The Tabernacle	68
The Embroidery	69
The Graven Image	70
The Specialist	71
The Cherubim	76

Six Wings	86
The Merkabah	88
The Ark Of The Covenant	91
A Dangerous Artifact	93
A Weapon	94
The Hornet	95
The Slow Killer	97
Shielding and Grounding	100
The Golden Calf	108
Other Technology	115
The Stone Tablets	121
Holographic Projection	126
Josua's recording stone	130
Comms	131
The Urim and Thummim	133
The Message	138
The 4th Kind: Abductions	**140**
Taking Captives	140
John	141
Enoch	144
Elijah	145
Ezekiel	147
Philip	148
Paul	149
Alien DNA	151
Nephilim	152
Noah	153
The Virgin Mary	159
Beware Barren Women Bearing Babies	162
Jesus	164

The 5th Kind - Inviting Contact	177
Summoning War	180
Summoning Peace	181
Conclusion	182
Appendices	183
Appendix A: A Chronology of Biblical UFO Encounters	183
Appendix B: Index of Bible Characters	185
Appendix C: Index of Hebrew Words	187
Appendix D: Ancient Hebrew, Dead Languages, and Hapax Legomena	190
About the Author	193
Further Resources	193

Introduction

In his groundbreaking book *Chariots of the Gods*, published in 1968, Erich Von Daniken discusses a handful of familiar bible tales from a rather unconventional perspective informed by the UFO phenomenon. Specifically mentioned are the tales of Sodom and Gomorrah, the visions of Ezekiel, and the design of the Ark of the Covenant.

It is the aim of this book to investigate the matter more thoroughly, and to reveal not merely a few, but literally dozens of biblical examples of UFO encounters. Topics such as giants, conspiracy theories, pyramids, secret societies, and ancient alien origins, though fascinating, and quite possibly relevant, are beyond the scope of this book. This book seeks to answer one question – what does the Bible have to say about UFO encounters.

The book is organized in a way to correspond generally with the Hynek scale, the de facto standard for classification of several "kinds" of UFO encounters. The scale was developed for the U.S. military program "Project Blue Book" by a physicist named Dr. J. Allen Hynek, who later became very well known as one the world leading ufologists.

In general, the encounters examined will be limited to the various types of "close encounters." Hynek argued that to suit a modicum of scientific rigour, only encounters occurring within about 500 feet of the observer could be trusted. This criteria greatly reduces the possibility of misidentifying conventional aircraft or other known phenomena. With one notable exception, all encounters discussed in this book are "close encounters." They are clear and present to the observer. They are physical phenomena, as indicated by physical evidence, physical description, or some other physical effect. Thus, they are subject to scientific study, though in many cases, the witness testimony may leave out many pertinent details.

A number of these cases have often been misrepresented as purely psychological or spiritual experiences. Certainly, the Bible contains many episodes of visions, dreams, or other states of altered consciousness. These may or may not have any relevance to extra-dimensional entities or extraterrestrial beings, however, in the absence of any textual indication of physical phenomenon, they are excluded from this investigation.

- Close Encounters of the First Kind are primarily visual sightings of an unidentified flying object, seemingly less than 500 feet away, that show considerable detail, rather than simply a light in the sky.
- Close Encounters of the Second Kind are UFO events in which a physical or physiological effect such as paralysis or heat and discomfort is alleged by the witness, or where some physical trace is produced, such as impressions in the ground, scorched vegetation etc.
- Close Encounters of the Third Kind involve an animated entity, whether humanoid or not, particularly any who appear to be associated with a UFO. Third Kind encounters often consist of an entity observed inside or nearby a UFO, often exiting or entering the vehicle. In some cases, an entity is observed, but no UFOs are seen by the observer. Perhaps UFO activity has been reported in the area by other witnesses at about the same time.
- A Close Encounter of the Fourth Kind is a UFO event in which a human is abducted by a UFO or its occupants. Witnesses may experience a transformation of their sense of reality.

- There exists an additional, more modern approach which has been labelled "the fifth kind". The differentiating factor here is who initiates the encounter rather than what types of phenomena are involved. For this reason, it is the opinion of this researcher that, although a useful categorization, it is really not an extension of the existing scale, but rather a different type of categorization altogether and one which does not fit terribly well into the structure of the Hynek scale. Nevertheless, it will be included into the scope of this book.

Hynek's scientific analyses seemed a good starting point for this investigation, and frankly, allows the book to proceed from a relatively benign position, only gradually adding more radical observations.

It should also be noted that this is not the first book intended to explore this fascinating subject. I know of several previously published works, including:

- Jessup, Morris K.; *UFO and the Bible*, 1956
- Paul Misraki; *Flying Saucers Through The Ages*, 1965
- Erich Von Daniken; *Chariots Of The Gods?*, 1968
- Barry Downing; *The Bible and Flying Saucers*, 1968
- Robert Dione; *God Drives a Flying Saucer*, 1969
- Josef F. Blumrich; *the Spaceships of Ezekiel*, 1974
- Rev. Michael J. S. Carter; *Alien Scriptures: Extraterrestrials in the Holy Bible*, 2013
- Xaviant Haze; *Ancient Aliens in the Bible*, 2017

During the preliminary research for this book, I became aware of these existing volumes, but purposed to avoid reading them while writing this book for the sake of avoiding any possible cross contamination. My aim was to prepare this book based solely on my own reading of scripture, without any undue influence from outside perspectives, however relevant or intriguing they may be. I look forward to reading these other fine books after publication of this volume and I would encourage you to do the same. It is always helpful to be open to other perspectives.

The 1st Kind: Visitations

Close Encounters of the First Kind are defined as visual sightings of an unidentified flying object, at a relatively close range, rather than simply a distant light in the sky. Having said that, by far the largest percentage of UFO sightings in modern times tend to be of the "not so close" kind. Aircraft, satellites, and even comets are regularly misidentified and reported as UFOs. These far-off encounters are notoriously and perniciously difficult to justify, particularly in modern day alleged UFO encounters, due to the fact that many ordinary objects can so easily be mistaken for so-called UFOs. In Biblical times however, there were of course no airplanes, satellites, weather balloons, and the like, although there certainly were comets and meteors which could sometimes present as lights in the sky, as well as even more distant objects in space, such as planets or celestial events such as supernovas. One notable case will be examined right off the bat, in order to get it out of the way. After which, all remaining cases will fall under the category of "close encounters", up close and personal, and with a high degree of scrutable witness reliability

The Three Wise Men

In the gospel of Matthew we read of "the three wise men": *...during the time of King Herod, Magi from the east came to Jerusalem and asked, "Where is the one who has been born king of the Jews? We saw his star when it rose and have come to worship him."*[1]

These men travelled a great distance, "following a star" as is traditionally summarized. This is much debated

---

[1] Matthew 2:1-2, New International Version

among scholars. Had these men, who were themselves ancient scholars, simply seen an omen in the sky which signalled them? Or was it something more than that? Were they literally following a moving object over a great distance for an extended period of time? Verse 9 answers our question.

...they went on their way, and the star they had seen when it rose went ahead of them until it stopped over the place where the child was.[2]

The passage clearly states that the object was still leading them, and that they were able to follow it on foot (or perhaps camel and donkey), even after a long journey. In fact, the Bible says that this object stopped over an exact location, such that the wise men were able to pinpoint the exact house it was indicating to them.

On coming to the house, they saw the child with his mother Mary, and they bowed down and worshiped him.[3]

A star in the sky cannot be traced to a specific house. A comet does not stop in its overhead journey. A supernova does not move across the sky. We are dealing with a glowing or shining object, similar to a star in appearance, that has the ability to stop and start, appears to be aware of the presence of its followers, such that it allows them to stop to speak to the king, and presumably to sleep each night on their journey, and then is able to pinpoint an exact house among many in the village. Did the object hover low over the house? Did the object send down a beam of light to shine upon the correct house? The passage does not say, but clearly there was some method of indication that could not be achieved by a distant star.

The witness testimony is recorded in the book of Matthew as an expert testimony. The author is explicit in describing the witnesses as wise scholars and seasoned

---

[2] Matthew 2:9, New International Version

[3] Matthew 2:11, New International Version

travellers from afar. These were no shepherds, though their story was corroborated by a group of shepherds nearby who also witnessed the flying lights. These were the J. Allen Hynek's of their day, the world-class scientists. Even though this object may very well be beyond the usual 500 feet limit, the extended time scale allowed for observation and the technical expertise of these expert witnesses make this a strong case.

Forty Years In The Desert

The "star" of the wise men is not the only instance of a shining object in the sky leading people. A large portion of the Old Testament takes place during the wanderings of the Hebrew people and their leader Moses, who were led for forty years by exactly such an object.

By day the Lord went ahead of them in a pillar of cloud to guide them on their way and by night in a pillar of fire to give them light, so that they could travel by day or night. Neither the pillar of cloud by day nor the pillar of fire by night left its place in front of the people.[4]

This phenomenon is described numerous times in the book of Exodus, and referred to in the books of Leviticus and Numbers. The pillar remains in full sight of the entire nation for forty years, until they finally reach their destination; the promised land of Canaan. The cloud goes over here; the crowd follows. The pillar moves this way; the nation trails behind. This may be the only way to comprehend why a large group of people would keep wandering back and forth for forty years rather than simply getting across the desert in a relatively straight line and getting on with their journey.

Although Exodus gives us a more detailed description than Matthew, the general behaviour of the

---

[4] Exodus 13:21-22, New International Version

object is eerily similar. The people are able to follow the object over vast distances throughout an extended timeframe.

In both cases, the object stops at a specific destination, and henceforth disappears from the narrative. Suddenly, when the Israelites reach their destination and the forty years has completed, the object seems to vanish. We do not hear of it again, at least not with the same description. We no longer hear of a pillar of fire or a pillar of cloud. Is it the end of the story? Perhaps not.

The 2nd Kind: Physical Evidence

Close Encounters of the Second Kind are UFO events in which a physical or physiological effect such as paralysis or heat and discomfort is alleged by the witness, or where some physical trace is produced, such as impressions in the ground, scorched vegetation etc.

Scorched Earth

The Bible contains more than a few stories of God smiting various people in sometimes very imaginative ways. You could say Yahweh has a bit of a reputation for it. In many of these cases, the texts are somewhat open to interpretation as possible UFO sightings. One such example is found in the eleventh chapter of the book of Numbers.

*Now the people complained about their hardships in the hearing of the Lord, and when he heard them his anger was aroused. Then **fire from the Lord burned among them and consumed some of the outskirts of the camp**. When the people cried out to Moses, he prayed to the Lord and the fire died down. So that place was called Taberah, because fire from the Lord had burned among them.*[5]

Granted, there is no direct mention of a UFO in this passage. Or is there? Actually, this is part of the same story of the pillar of fire and the pillar of cloud. One fact that is often overlooked by bible readers is that the chapter breaks are not part of the original text. Chapter 11 of the book of Numbers is simply a continuation of the text in chapter 10. In reality, the burning of the camp occurs immediately after another mention of the pillar of fire and cloud.

---

[5] Numbers 11:1-3

The cloud of the Lord was over them by day when they set out from the camp.[6]

It seems that the fire was caused by a close brush with the pillar of fire. The interesting thing here is that only the outskirts of the camp were touched by the fire. This was perhaps not a purposeful punishment from an all powerful divine being. It was more like a glancing blow, an unplanned reaction, almost a flippant response. If God was trying to smite the people, he did a really lousy job. This was more like a scare tactic that got a little too close and accidentally caused some singeing. This huge flaming object swooped down from the sky, getting a little too close. There was a good reason the people usually stayed far back from the pillar of fire.

Two Camps

In Genesis chapter thirty-two, we read of two separate encounters experienced by Jacob, the son of Isaac, and grandson of Abraham. The chapter begins:

Jacob also went on his way, and the angels of God met him. When Jacob saw them, he said, "This is the camp of God!" So he named that place Mahanaim.[7]

Here is Jacob's first encounter. Very little detail is given, but Jacob witnessed something which caused him to name the place 'Two Camps'.

Who exactly did he meet? The Hebrew words used here are מַלְאֲכֵי אֱלֹהִים (pronounced 'malake elohim') which gets translated as 'angels of God', and מַחֲנֵה אֱלֹהִים (pronounced 'mahaneh elohim') which is typically translated as the 'camp of God.'

The word 'malakeh' means 'messengers'. The use of the English word 'angels' is actually quite misleading in

---

[6] Numbers 10:34
[7] Genesis 32:1-2

this context. This word 'malakeh' is used many times throughout the Bible to indicate messengers, regardless of their physical characteristics or their origin. Messengers are often dispatched with letters or gifts from someone just as couriers are still used today. There is nothing about the word 'malakeh' that indicates an angel or any other kind of supernatural being.

The word 'mananeh' is also used many times in the Old Testament, and does generally mean camp. Interestingly, though, it can also be used to mean 'army'. This is not surprising, since an army generally does use a camp for its rest stops. However, when paired with the fact that 'elohim' is a plural noun, rather than a proper noun, the meaning begins to shift somewhat. 'The camps of the elohim', or 'the armies of the elohim' both clearly convey the idea of a host of living individuals who have settled somewhere for the night. Even though Jacob does not record any detailed descriptions of what these beings were like, the event made an impression on him, and he made a point of naming the place after these unusual visitors. Unfortunately, this very brief mention does not give any indications as to who exactly was camped out here. We know only that Jacob stayed at this spot for a night or two, but soon sent his family ahead to stay with his brother. Once alone, Jacob describes another encounter, this one more detailed and a bit stranger than the last.

So Jacob was left alone, and a man wrestled with him till daybreak. When the man saw that he could not overpower him, he touched the socket of Jacob's hip so that his hip was wrenched as he wrestled with the man. Then the man said, "Let me go, for it is daybreak."

But Jacob replied, "I will not let you go unless you bless me."

The man asked him, "What is your name?"

"Jacob," he answered.

Then the man said, "Your name will no longer be Jacob, but Israel, because you have struggled with God and with humans and have overcome."

Jacob said, "Please tell me your name."

But he replied, "Why do you ask my name?" Then he blessed him there.

So Jacob called the place Peniel, saying, "It is because I saw God face to face, and yet my life was spared."

*The sun rose above him as he passed Peniel, and **he was limping because of his hip**. Therefore to this day the Israelites do not eat the tendon attached to the socket of the hip, because the socket of Jacob's hip was touched near the tendon.*[8]

There are a few key points to be made here. In verse 24, *"a man wrestled with him until daybreak"*. However, the word 'man' clearly does not mean a human, for as has already been established, Jacobs visitors have already been identified as 'angels' or more correctly, as the messengers of the elohim, or the armies of the elohim. A closer look at the text reveals that the Hebrew word אִישׁ (pronounced 'ish'), does not mean man or human at all. In fact, in nearly every biblical instance except this verse, the word is translated as 'another'. The implication here is that of difference. Jacob wrestled with some kind of different being: 'an other'. Indeed, for it was no man. This 'other' goes on to ask Jacob his name, but purposely withholds his own name, as though irrelevant. This is not the all-knowing Yahweh. This messenger of the elohim seems to have been sent to give Jacob a new name, which he does. 'Israel', or as verse 28 tells us, "you have struggled and prevailed with both anasim and elohim". 'Anasim' generally translates as 'men', but it is always in reference to one's own men; their warriors, their best spies, even their husbands. The

---

[8] Genesis 32:24-32, New International Version

implication of "anasim and elohim" is indeed that of two camps. Jacob's own kind, and the other kind; the elohim. And so Jacob becomes known as he who has prevailed in struggle against both his own kind as well as 'the others'.

So Jacob called the place Peniel, saying, "It is because I saw God face to face, and yet my life was spared."

Again we must dig into the Hebrew text. Notice again the use of the term 'elohim'. Rather than "I saw God face to face" this phrase is more accurately translated as "I saw the elohim face to face." Even in his summary, Jacob does not claim to have fought GOD or Yahweh or any other name other than "the elohim". He might just as well have said "I fought an alien and lived to tell the tale." This was certainly a life-altering event worth talking about. Is it any wonder then, that hereafter Jacob became known by a new nickname?

We conclude this segment on Jacob with a final point. This is the reason that this encounter can be categorized as being of "the Second Kind". Jacob was left with physical evidence of his encounter in the form of an injury. He now walked with a limp, the result of his strenuous physical activity wrestling with a physical and quite capable opponent.

The 3rd Kind: Beings & Communications

As mentioned in the introduction, Close Encounters of the Third Kind involve an animated entity, particularly any who appear to be occupants or pilots of a UFO.

Further third kind subcategorizations were developed by Ted Bloecher, cofounder of the Civilian Saucer Intelligence of New York and a member of the National Investigations Committee on Aerial Phenomena, and the Center for UFO Studies. His proposed subtypes are as follows:

-Subtype A (Aboard) : An entity is observed only inside the UFO.
-Subtype B (Both) : An entity is observed inside and outside the UFO.
-Subtype C (Close) : An entity is observed near to a UFO, but not going in or out.
-Subtype D (Direct) : An entity is observed, but no UFOs are seen by the observer. UFO activity has been reported in the area at about the same time.
-Subtype E (Excluded) : An entity is observed, but no UFOs are seen or reported in the vicinity.
-Subtype F (Frequence) : No entity or UFOs are observed, but the subject experiences some sort of "intelligent communication".

Each of these subtypes are well represented within the Biblical literature, as shall be seen in the following chapters.

Jacob's Ladder

In the previous chapter two UFO encounters were examined as witnessed by Jacob and recounted in Genesis chapter 32.

We will now jump backwards to an earlier part of Jacob's story, and a very well known part at that. Genesis 28 tells the story that is commonly known today as "Jacob's ladder".

Jacob left Beersheba and set out for Harran. When he reached a certain place, he stopped for the night because the sun had set. Taking one of the stones there, he put it under his head and lay down to sleep. He had a dream in which he saw a stairway resting on the earth, with its top reaching to heaven, and the angels of God were ascending and descending on it. There above it stood the Lord, and he said: "I am the Lord, the God of your father Abraham and the God of Isaac. I will give you and your descendants the land on which you are lying. Your descendants will be like the dust of the earth, and you will spread out to the west and to the east, to the north and to the south. All peoples on earth will be blessed through you and your offspring. I am with you and will watch over you wherever you go, and I will bring you back to this land. I will not leave you until I have done what I have promised you."

This story is set in the context of a dream. We do not know if Jacob was literally dreaming, or if he was simply sleeping until some strange event awoke him. However, there is ample reason to conclude that perhaps it was not just a dream. Reading further, we see Jacob's rather extreme reaction.

When Jacob awoke from his sleep, he thought, "Surely the Lord is in this place, and I was not aware of it." He was afraid and said, "How awesome is this place! This is none other than the house of God; this is the gate of heaven."

Early the next morning Jacob took the stone he had placed under his head and set it up as a pillar and poured oil on top of it. He called that place Bethel, though the city used to be called Luz.

Then Jacob made a vow, saying, "If God will be with me and will watch over me on this journey I am taking and will give me food to eat and clothes to wear so that I return safely to my father's household, then the Lord will be my God and this stone that I have set up as a pillar will be God's house, and of all that you give me I will give you a tenth."

Firstly, Jacob is amazed. Why? Has he never had a dream before? Surely this is not true, for he is a grown man. Furthermore, Jacob goes on to perform a sacred ritual, anointing and commemorating the location and naming it. Was Jacob in the custom of performing such rituals every time he had a dream? He goes on to swear a solemn oath, and a very life changing one at that. He swears to give back a tenth of his income, thus initiating a tradition of tithing that is followed to this day by millions of Christians, and involving billions of dollars annually. This is no meagre thing. Why would Jacob do all of this, just because he had a dream? It seems that this experience was something more. Something more real than a dream.

Now let us examine the details of the "dream".

he saw a stairway resting on the earth, with its top reaching to heaven,

The Hebrew word סֻלָּם (pronounced sulam) is used only once in the entire bible. We do not really know what it means. The next word is מֻצָּב (pronounced mussab) is used in only one other location, where it is translated as "of the pillar" or "at the pillar". next we have אַרְצָה (arsah) which is a common word meaning land or ground. The next phrase is as follows; וְרֹאשׁוֹ (werosow) always translates to "head", מַגִּיעַ (maggia) usually translated as "arrived", and finally הַשָּׁמָיְמָה (hassamayema) meaning "to/from/of the sky".

It seems somewhat dishonest to assume that we know something we don't and inject the english words "ladder" or "stairway" into this story. It is more honest and accurate to simply say that Jacob saw "something" and that it was somehow related to or acting upon the ground. Could it have been some unknown object landing on the ground? All we really know is that "a thing did something on or to the ground." We also see that it is connected somehow to the sky. Perhaps it stretched to the sky or perhaps it came from the sky. All of this to say that there are two equally feasible ways to interpret this sentence. It is just as fair to say:

"he saw a strange object land on the ground whose head arrived from the sky."

We are not one hundred percent certain that this object is a flying one, but we know for sure that it is both an object, and unidentified.

Next, we see some beings:

and the angels of God were ascending and descending on it. There above it stood the Lord, and he said: "I am the Lord, the God of your father Abraham and the God of Isaac

These so-called "angels" are the same "malake" or messengers, that we already witnessed in Jacob's other encounters. This sentence is very difficult to translate, for it contains two words which appear nowhere else in the Bible, and one which gets translated into so many different words that it seems to rely entirely on context and bring almost no meaning of its own. About the best we can do is a very loose translation as follows:

"The messengers of the elohim, עֹלִים (olim) went up, וְיֹרְדִים בּוֹ:(weyoredim bo) (two more unused words whose meaning is unknown) and behold Yahweh stood עָלָיו (alaw) (too contextual to translate)."

There are a lot of unknowns in this account, but it could be interpreted as some sort of unusual non-human but seemingly humanoid looking beings, on or in some sort of structure or craft in the sky, with someone identifying themself as Yahweh and giving Jacob a message. Whatever it was, it was a life-changing moment for Jacob, and no mere dream.

Wheels Within Wheels

The first chapter of the book of Ezekiel is a very bizarre section of literature. It appears to be a description of an experience that the prophet Ezekiel had one day. However, his descriptive narrative seems to jump around and includes many elements which appear contradictory and perhaps deliberately obtuse or obfuscating. Could it be that some of the semantic problems we see here are the result of unsatisfactory translation efforts? We have already seen some rather difficult-to-interpret passages within the Jacob narrative. Is it possible that Ezekiel 1 contains several gross misrepresentations or misapplications of the Hebrew lexicon? Are there other possible translations of this passage which may elucidate a greater understanding and a clearer depiction of what Ezekiel was witnessing? This may in fact be the case. Furthermore, Ezekiel's first encounter is somewhat lengthy, taking up the better part of three chapters, so rather than belabor the point it may be prudent to present a summarized paraphrase with a few explanatory notes on certain key points of translation.

The first three verses of Ezekiel specify his location and the exact time and date of the encounter. This is important to note as it grounds the narrative to a specific, real, physical event. Ezekiel is describing a real encounter that he experienced.

In my thirtieth year, in the fourth month on the fifth day, while I was among the exiles by the Kebar River, the heavens were opened and I saw visions of God.[9]

The final phrase of the opening verse could also be translated "the sky opened, and I saw the sight of the elohim". The Hebrew word for sky refers to a physical location rather than a conceptual realm. "The sky" is a more accurate translation than "the heavens". The Hebrew word for open implies allowing, breaking forth, expressing, loosening, releasing. The sky was releasing something. "I saw the sight" is a more accurate description than "vision". The term vision in this context incorrectly implies a metaphysical phenomenon. There is nothing in the text of this passage to indicate that a supernatural occurrence is happening. Ezekiel describes his current physical location and time, then goes on to describe a physical event that he witnessed. He saw these things happening. He is not in a trance or dream state. It is not some kind of psychedelic hallucination. It is a real thing that he saw, that is strange and that he tries very hard but with no small amount of difficulty to adequately describe.

The elohim is a plural denotation for a type of being. It is typically translated as "God" but in no way does it imply a singular personality or any of the divine attributes carried by the English word God. Ezekiel did not see one God. He saw several beings. These beings are described in greater detail below.

On the fifth of the month—it was the fifth year of the exile of King Jehoiachin—the word of the Lord came to Ezekiel the priest, the son of Buzi, by the Kebar River in the land of the Babylonians. There the hand of the Lord was on him.[10]

---

[9] Ezekiel 1:1, New International Version

[10] Ezekiel 1:2-3, New International Version

A more accurate translation may be:

In the fifth day of the month, which was the fifth year of King Jehoiachin's captivity, *a message from Yahweh* was delivered to Ezekiel the priest, son of Buzi, in the land of the Chaldeans by the river Chebar, and *there the hand of Yahweh came.*

Ezekiel now uses the direct name of God, Yahweh. The message is relayed to him by the elohim who have appeared. "A message from Yahweh" thus is a more accurate translation than "the word of the lord". Some translations use a passive verb "came" and others acknowledge a more active verb "came expressly." A Ezekiel is explicitly describing the process by which the message was delivered.

In the land may also be interpreted "on the ground" thus again emphasizing the physical nature of the phenomenon described. Notice the details of the physical location.

"and there the hand of Yahweh came". This phrase includes several important elements. Overall, it is a summary of the entire event, something came from the sky. Ezekiel dubs it "the hand of Yahweh". Again the proper name for God is used here. As the message is understood as being from God, so the method of its delivery is also recognized thusly. The hand is a physical manifestation that performs action. The hand is the power of intention made real. Some translations use "the hand of the lord was upon him there." This is less fitting for two reasons. Firstly, "the lord" is a watered down title rather than the proper name Yahweh which is used in the original language. Secondly the phrase "upon him" is not included or implied in the Hebrew. Rather it is injected spontaneously into the English translation. "Upon him" incorrectly implies a state of mind. The phrase is commonly recognized in a broader context used elsewhere in scripture: "the spirit of the lord came upon him". This phrase implies trance-like altered consciousness which does not belong in this context. There is no justification for an attempt to read this text as a metaphysical treatise. It is a simple description of a physical event. A physical object appeared, bringing a message from Yahweh. This summarizes the thesis of Ezekiel's testimony. He then moves on to a detailed description.

I looked, and I saw a windstorm coming out of the north—an immense cloud with flashing lightning and surrounded by brilliant light. The center of the fire looked like glowing metal.[11]

A more literal interpretation of "windstorm" would be "a violent spirit", but this phrase may certainly be interpreted as a strong and stormy wind. The north is probably meant as the literal direction, but also carries with it cultural hints of symbology referring to invaders and exile. Similarly, the word used for cloud here may also connote invasion and gloom. from this gloom flashes forth fire and light. Another translation points out the bright metallic nature of the light; *"a great cloud with flashing fire and brightness all around it, and something like a glowing alloy out of the fire."*[12]

Ezekiel sees a sudden billowing of thick clouds with lights shooting from within, then something emerges. Something shiny and metallic. A metallic object in the sky from which four humanoid creatures exit. What else could you call this but some type of ship?

The rest of chapter one consists of three distinct descriptive sections, each focusing on one of three specific physical elements of this experience: the humanoid creatures, the shining man, and the machinations of the ship itself. Chapter two relays the message that the shining man gives to Ezekiel. Chapter three concludes the message and relates the departure of the ship.

---

[11] Ezekiel 1:4, New International Version
[12] Ezekiel 1:4, Tree Of Life Version

It may be beneficial to take the liberty of rearranging the text slightly, moving the machinery section to precede the section describing the humanoid creatures. We have seen only the quickest glimpse of a shining metal object. Why not examine it in more detail before moving onto its inhabitants.

I saw a wheel on the ground beside each creature with its four faces. This was the appearance and structure of the wheels: They sparkled like topaz, and all four looked alike. Each appeared to be made like a wheel intersecting a wheel.[13]

Their rims were high and awesome, and all four rims were full of eyes all around.[14]

The word for wheel used here is אוֹפַן (owpan). The same word is used in the Bible to describe both the wheels of chariots and for large circular grinding stones used in the process of grinding grain. Grinding stones may be configured in either vertical or horizontal configurations, depending on the type of grain, the size of the stone, and the type of manpower or ox-power available. The salient feature of an 'owpan' is that it is round. There is an extra association with the English word 'wheel' that is not necessarily implied or apropos. We are so used to wheels on cars and trucks and bicycles that we do not imagine them in any other configuration. We should not assume that it must be a vertically oriented wheel with one point touching the ground.

This orientation is in no way implied in the original text. What we should read here is that Ezekiel saw four round objects. They may have been upright like a wheel, or they may have been horizontal like a disk laying flat.

However, both grinding stones and wheels share another characteristic. They turn, or spin. In the case of a

---

[13] Ezekiel 1:15-16, New International Version

[14] Ezekiel 1:18, New International Version

grinding stone, it is generally a much slower motion than the spinning of a wheel. This spinning motion will be examined more closely shortly.

Ezekiel also indicates that these round objects are now "on the ground". This word is בָּאָרֶץ (ba-ares). Notably, it is not the same word for ground used in the Jacob's Ladder story. That word was אַרְצָה (arsah), which means ground or land. Here we encounter a different word בָּאָרֶץ (ba-ares). "Ba-ares" has a different connotation. It is usually translated "on the earth" but carries with it the implication of the physical realm, rather than simply the ground or the land. For example, in Genesis 1:22 the word is used to describe the realm of birds. "let birds multiply on the earth." Clearly, birds are creatures of the sky, and even when they nest, they do so above the ground in the treetops. Another example of this word is in Genesis 6:5 *"The Lord saw how great the wickedness of the human race had become on the earth, and that every inclination of the thoughts of the human heart was only evil all the time."* Here, it is clear that earth is used to differentiate between the world of mankind, and the other world of God. It has nothing to do with the ground itself in the sense of dirt and bedrock. Rather than saying that the round objects are on "the ground", what Ezekiel is conveying here is that these objects came "to earth".

Ezekiel then describes the appearance of these round objects further. The words used here indicate gemstones, but nothing can be inferred about the color per se, for the same gemstone's name can be applied to a wide variety of gems from topaz to beryl to rubies or emeralds. The various Bible translations are correctly indistinct in their ability to determine between color and sparkle.

One translation says *"They sparkled like topaz"*[15], while another says *"the appearance of the wheels and their*

---

[15] Ezekiel 1:16, New International Version

workings was like the color of beryl"[16] What we can infer here is that the objects seemed to have a gem-like quality, most likely involving some kind of sparkling appearance. Could it be that the craft were fitted with flashing lights? An important word in this phrase is omitted from many translations. We have seen it included in the New King James Version, to the translator's credit. This is the Hebrew word וּמַעֲשֵׂיהֶם (uma-asehem) which means works, deeds, workings, or machinery. Certainly, lights would fit into this category. However, this may also refer to the next fascinating characteristic of this object, the one for which it has become famous, the so-called "wheels within wheels".

The keyword here is the Hebrew word בְּתוֹךְ (betowk). In many other Bible verses it is typically translated "among or in the midst".

There is a range of subtle differences within various of the standard Bible translations.

- "a wheel within a wheel" is by far the most commonly chosen interpretation, favored by the English Standard Version, Berean Study Bible, Christian Standard Bible, and Holman Christian Standard Bible.

- "as if one wheel were within another" is used by the New American Standard Bible, and the International Standard Version.

- "a wheel in the middle of a wheel." says the King James Bible, and New King James Version.

Some translations add more geometric details of the configuration, such as:

---

[16] Ezekiel 1:16, New King James Version

"a wheel intersecting a wheel"	New International Version
"another wheel intersecting it at right angles"	Good News Translation
"a second wheel turning crosswise within it"	New Living Translation
"Each wheel was exactly the same and had a second wheel that cut through the middle of it"	Contemporary English Version

These translations appear to be based less on the original Hebrew scripture, and more on the teachings of later Jewish merkabah mysticism cults, which shall be discussed further in a later chapter.

Many of these configurations are difficult to imagine as solid objects. Suppose however that the reference to the gem-like flashing lights and the reference to the wheels among or in the midst of other wheels are actually referring to a single aspect of the ship. Of course they are. It is a single short verse in which we find both references.

"The appearance of the wheels and their craftsmanship was like the gleam of beryl, and all four had the same form. Their appearance and craftsmanship was like a wheel within a wheel."[17]

---

[17] Ezekiel 1:16, Holman Christian Standard Bible

It now becomes easy to envision the flashing lights moving in concentric circular patterns around the edge of the ship and in a smaller circle within that.

Finally, there is one more detail to consider.

Their rims were high and awesome, and all four rims were full of eyes all around.[18]

The Hebrew word וְגַבֵּיהֶן (wegabbehen) is an uncommon word which may mean defenses or armor[19], rather than "rim" which is the typical translation here. The Hebrew word וְיִרְאָה (weyirah) is probably better translate as "fearsome".[20] Thus, a more accurate translation would be "The high and fearsome armor, was full of eyes roundabout".

Interestingly, we have already touched upon the metallic and gleaming nature of the craft, and the idea of a ring of lights around its circumference. This last clue seems to tie it all together. Surely "eyes" are a suitable metaphor from someone who has never seen electric lights before. In fact, the word for eyes, עֵינַיִם (enayim) is generally used metaphorically throughout the Bible, referring to the soul, one's perception. one's general appearance, the mind, and general understanding or even sapience.

Regarding the motion of the objects, Ezekiel takes pains to try to explain that each ship was with a living being, and that the being was inside the ship, and that somehow, inexplicably to Ezekiel, the living creatures were somehow controlling the movement of the ships. He makes it clear that the ships themselves were not rotating, even though they seemed to have a rotating pattern of lights on them. The ships flew in straight lines, wherever the pilot wanted. To Ezekiel, this was a mind-blowing concept. The only vehicles he had ever seen were pulled slowly by horses

---

[18] Ezekiel 1:18, New International Version
[19] see Job 15:26, Job 13:12, Ezekiel 43:13, Ezekiel 16:24
[20] see Job 6:14, Proverbs 1:29, Isaiah 11:2

or oxen or other animals with a mind of their own who would often stray from the path, requiring constant steering adjustments.

As they moved, they would go in any one of the four directions the creatures faced; the wheels did not change direction as the creatures went.[21]

Whenever the living beings moved, the wheels moved with them. And whenever the living beings rose from the earth, the wheels rose also. Wherever the spirit was about to go, they would go in that direction. And the wheels rose close beside them; for the spirit of the living beings was in the wheels. Whenever those went, these went; and whenever those stood still, these stood still. And whenever those rose from the earth, the wheels rose close beside them; for the spirit of the living beings was in the wheels.[22]

He also takes notice of the sounds made by the objects. At the initial appearance of the clouds, there were loud storm-like thunderings. As the objects approach, he now describes their sound again *"I heard the sound of their wings, like the roar of rushing waters, like the voice of the Almighty, like the tumult of an army. When they stood still, they lowered their wings."*[23] This sounds very much like some type of engine, particularly the detail that the sound seems to wind down as they lower their wings.

Inside the object, Ezekiel says, *was what looked like four living creatures. In appearance their form was human*[24]

The use of the Hebrew word דְּמוּת (demut) meaning image or likeness may indicate that the creatures were not viewed directly but that they were visible through a window

---

[21] Ezekiel 1:17, New International Version
[22] Ezekiel 1:19-21, New American Standard Version
[23] Ezekiel 1:24, New International Version
[24] Ezekiel 1:5, New International Version

of some sort. These beings' appearance was the מַרְאֵיהֶן (marahen) "resemblance" of a human.

Ezekiel is clear that the creatures resemble humans. But what follows in most translations is anything but human-like. Could this be due to flaws in the translation or interpretation?

"each of them had four faces and four wings."[25] Every major English translation uses the same words, four faces and four wings. With such unanimous agreement among translators, one would almost think that the Hebrew words were obvious and easy to translate. However, this is not the case at all.

The word translated as faces is the Hebrew word פָּנִים (panim). This word is used to represent a wide variety of concepts. In other Bible verses it is translated as persons/people, regard/respect/honor, acceptance, another, man, and edge.[26]

Even within Ezekiel's own writing, the word appears to have several meanings. In Ezekiel 2:4 the shining man tells him "I am sending you to them who are *stubborn and obstinate* children."[27] This is the same word, "panim". So Ezekiel is given a message to give to the "panim" children, and he sees four creatures with four "panims". What word can possibly fit into both these spots? Ecclesiastes 10:10 may shed some light on the matter. It says "If the axe is dull and he does not sharpen its edge, then he must exert more strength"[28] Here "panim" is translated to "edge". This might actually work in Ezekiel's case as well.

---

[25] Ezekiel 1:6, New International Version

[26] Deuteronomy 1:17, Deuteronomy 10:17, Deuteronomy 28:50, 2 Kings 5:1, 2 Kings 14:8, 2 Kings 14:11, 2 Chronicles 19:7, Job 22:8, Isaiah 3:3, Isaiah 9:15

[27] Ezekiel 2:4, New American Standard Bible

[28] Ecclesiastes 10:10, New American Standard Bible

Ezekiel 2:4 becomes "I am sending you to them who are *sharp-edged* children." and Ezekiel 1:5 now reads "each of them had four *edges* and four wings". It is still not entirely clear what is meant here, however we appear to be moving in the direction of greater internal consistency. Can a humanoid figure have four edges? What this means is not obvious, but it is relatively easy to imagine some type of garment or suit which appears to have four edges. This may also account for the inclusion of wings. Perhaps edges and wings are two words describing the same thing; some aspect of their appearance or their clothing or apparatus. This supposition is further strengthened by the fact that the word for wings also has a similar connotation. This word used here is כְּנָפַיִם (kenapayim) which is derived from כָּנָף (kanap). In general, "kanap" is literally a wing, on a bird or in statuary. However, In 1 Samuel 24:5, when David cuts "the edge of Saul's robe" it is his "kanap". This solidifies both the interpretation of a wing as a hem or edge, and the association with a part of a garment.

This certainly seems to make more sense than a humanoid with four heads or faces. Even the strangest non-humanoid biological curiosities may have many legs or other odd body compositions, but there are none that have multiple heads. Thus it seems that a better interpretation of verse six would be not *"each of them had four faces and four wings."*, but rather "each of them had four edges."

Verse 7 briefly mentions the legs and feet, which will be addressed momentarily. Verse 8 continues the description of the "edges", by adding that the hands of a human were under each of their four edges. The word וִידֵי (wi-de) is sometimes used literally to mean hands, but it also can have a geometrical implication, or the implication of the works of man, or the rule of man.

In Exodus 17:12, "Moses' hands were heavy" means he was tired of his laborious work. In Psalm 141:6, "wi-de" is translated "the sides"[29] or "places"[30]. Jeremiah 10:9 uses the word to convey the concept of handiwork, artistically skilled design and craft. The next word מִתַּחַת (mittahat) generally means under, and again, this word is often used figurative for concepts such a dominion[31] or foundation[32], just as "under" implies even still in English. "The hands of a human were under each of their four edges." may actually mean that the craftsmanship of the creature's suits appeared to be of human origin (as far as he could tell). In other words, Ezekiel may be pointing out that the garments worn by the four creatures are technological objects, rather than naturally occurring objects and contrasted to the normal type of woven textile garments he was familiar with. It appears to be "man-made". This is further bolstered by the next phrase. He points out that their edges, or "wings" touched one another. In terms of an object with edges, it is obvious that the edges touch each other. This mathematical surety is what allows a solid object to take form. Ezekiel's observation further strengthens both the geometrical implications inherent in "wi-de" and the foundational and design underpinnings suggested by "mittahat".

Using the assumption that faces and wings can be interpreted as "edges", verse ten goes on to describe these edges. Each suited creature had four edges, upon which can be seen certain forms. There is the face of a human, probably the humanoid creature's actual face, possibly seen through a face shield, as we have here the same "image" disclaimer as when seen through the window in verse 5. The right edge somehow resembles a lion, the left somehow

---

[29] New American Standard Bible

[30] King James Version

[31] Deuteronomy 5:8, Deuteronomy 7:24, 1 Kings 8:23, 2 Kings 13:5, 2 Kings 17:7

[32] Exodus 30:4, Exodus 37:27, 1 Kings 7:24, 1 Kings 7:30

resembles a bull. There is also the resemblance of an eagle in an unspecified location. These images are signified by the word וּדְמוּת, (udemut) which is used only in 2 Chronicles 4:3, describing bronze castings in the image of bulls which are built into a large round bronze ceremonial altar in the Hebrew temple. The only two uses of the word in the Bible both refer to a pattern of bull images around the edge of a large round metallic object of some importance. Could this be a coincidence? It may be important to realize that the lion/ox/bull/man adjuncture is not unique to Ezekiel's experience. Ezekiel was one of the many Hebrews who were captured by the Babylonian Empire and taken to live in Mesopotamia, a land also known as Assyria, Sumer, or Iraq. One of the most common motifs found in the art and statuary of this region is the lamassu. The lamassu is a celestial being from the ancient religion of the region bearing a human head, bull's body, wings like an eagle and sometimes a mane-like hairdo or large beard resembling a lion's mane. At the risk of veering into the territory of Sumerian scholar Zecharia Sitchin, it must be mentioned that perhaps there does appear to be some type of connection here, but it is beyond the scope of this book to speculate further about such theories.

    Aside from simply covering their bodies, the four edges of the suits are said to stretch out above, and two edges from each touch one of the creatures. Again, one could speculate at great length on the up-stretching edges and what sounds like connections between the creatures, but without any further detail given, such speculation seems unfounded.

    A further detail is mentioned in verse 7 regarding the feet and legs of the creatures. Ezekiel tells us that their legs are straight, their feet somewhat clunky like hooves, and that they appeared to be clad in some type of metallic boot. At this point it almost becomes trivial to picture a technological suit of some kind being somewhat bulky to walk in, just as modern spacesuits are.

Verse 13 tells of the luminous quality of the creatures:

The appearance of the living creatures was like burning coals of fire or like torches. Fire moved back and forth among the creatures; it was bright, and lightning flashed out of it. The creatures sped back and forth like flashes of lightning.[33]

There appears to be bright light both in or on, as well as between the creatures, with rapid flashes of light. Ezekiel's description is reminiscent of a jittery holographic projection. *Spread out above the heads of the living creatures was what looked something like a vault, sparkling like crystal, and awesome.*[34] Could this vault be background data of some kind of holographic projection?

Now a fifth object appears above the four: it looks like a throne made of sapphire. *Above the vault over their heads was what looked like a throne of ...*[35] sapphire. A sparkling blue gemstone. Many popular translations have, for some unknown reason, changed this from a sapphire, to a much less impressive lapis-lazuli. Lapis-lazuli is a very intensely blue stone which is beautiful in its own right, much as jade is prized for its intense green color. However lapis-lazuli is not a gem. That is, it lacks the shining translucent qualities of gemstones. To switch out this word is puzzling to say the least. The Hebrew word is סַפִּיר. It is pronounced "sappir". It is literally the word from which the English word sapphire is directly derived. There is no doubt of what this throne looked like. It was not a simple blue rock, but a gleaming, glittering sapphire. Ezekiel spells it out for us, yet some translators somewhere in history seem

---

[33] Ezekiel 1:13-14, New International Version
[34] Ezekiel 1:22, New International Version
[35] Ezekiel 1:26, New International Version

to have decided it best to substitute the completely obvious word. Were they under some compulsion or agenda to make it sound more mundane?

Seated on this brilliant sparkling throne is what appears to be a man. *High above, on the throne was a figure like that of a man.* The word used here for man is אָדָם (adam). You will no doubt recognize the word from the story of Adam and Eve. Yes, it's the same word. Adam is not actually a proper name, but rather it is the word for "human". The person sitting on this sapphire throne appears to be a human. However, there are certain rather non-human qualities about him.

I saw that from what appeared to be his waist up he looked like glowing metal, as if full of fire, and that from there down he looked like fire; and brilliant light surrounded him. Like the appearance of a rainbow in the clouds on a rainy day, so was the radiance around him. This was the appearance of the likeness of the glory of the Lord.[36] Ezekiel actually uses the name of God here, Yahweh. Lord is a poor translation fueled by a common practice following a desire to keep the name of God holy by not uttering it. Strangely though, the man has already been identified as human in the preceding verse. Ezekiel could have just as easily said that an elohim sat on the throne. Instead he used the word אָדָם, "adam", the designator for humans. Is Ezekiel confused? Understandably so. Clearly, Ezekiel identifies this glowing metallic rainbow human as his own God, Yahweh.

"When I saw it, I fell facedown," says Ezekiel. He was not simply hiding his face in the ground. He was worshipping the glowing man. This is no minor point. The penalty for worshipping other gods was death. Although Ezekiel had just seen a lot of weird and confusing stuff, in the end he makes up his mind. This must be God himself.

---

[36] Ezekiel 1:26-28, New International Version

He then hears a voice, apparently coming from the glowing man: *there came a voice from above the vault over their heads as they stood with lowered wings.*[37] *[...] and I heard the voice of one speaking.*[38]

This voice delivers a message to Ezekiel; a message which he is to relay to his countrymen, his fellow Hebrews living in Babylon. The message is lengthy and rife with all manner of religious and political connotations which are well beyond the scope of this book. After receiving the message, Ezekiel describes the departing of the creatures in their crafts, with much roaring of engines as they lifted off.

Then the Spirit lifted me up, and I heard behind me a loud rumbling sound as the glory of the Lord rose from the place where it was standing. It was the sound of the wings of the living creatures brushing against each other and the sound of the wheels beside them, a loud rumbling sound. The Spirit then lifted me up and took me away, and I went in bitterness and in the anger of my spirit, with the strong hand of the Lord on me. I came to the exiles who lived at Tel Aviv near the Kebar River. And there, where they were living, I sat among them for seven days—deeply distressed.[39]

Oddly, he includes a few strange phrases: "the spirit lifted me up", and "The Spirit then lifted me up and took me away", and "the strong hand of the Lord on me". These phrases may cause one to ponder if perhaps Ezekiel was taken up into the craft temporarily. Perhaps the only fact we can be sure of is that this event clearly appears to be a close encounter of the Third Kind. There appears to be several disk-like spacecraft, from which emerge the presence of humanoid beings. After the incident, Ezekiel is shaken, and can only sit in deep distress for seven days.

---

[37] Ezekiel 1:25, New International Version
[38] Ezekiel 1:28, New International Version
[39] Ezekiel 3:12-15, New International Version

Better Translations

All in all, this is a strange story, and it is difficult to say with any certainty what Ezekiel really saw. However, the existing standard translations seem only to add unnecessary obfuscation. Thus a more accurate translation is presented:

In my thirtieth year, in the fourth month on the fifth day, while I was among the exiles by the Kebar River, the sky opened, and I saw the sight of the elohim.

In the fifth day of the month, which was the fifth year of King Jehoiachin's captivity, a message from Yahweh was delivered to Ezekiel the priest, son of Buzi, on the ground of the Chaldeans by the river Chebar, and there the hand of Yahweh came.

I looked, and I saw a violent spirit coming out of the north—an immense cloud with flashing lightning and surrounded by brilliant light. In the center it looked like glowing metal.

I saw four round objects come to earth, each with a humanoid creature within it, driving it.

All four were high and fearsome. Their armour and their craftsmanship had circular patterns which spun independently of the object's direction of travel, and sparkled like gemstones, giving the impression of eyes roundabout.

The object moved wherever their pilot took them. They did not stray from their course and they could go in any direction including up and down. They were noisy like a roaring waterfall, like the din of an army, like the voice of the Almighty.

Inside each of the four objects was a being resembling a human. Each had the face of a human. Each of them had four edges. The hands of a human were under each of their four edges. Their edges touched one another. The right edge somehow resembled a lion, the left somehow resembled a bull. There was also the resemblance of an eagle.

Aside from simply covering their bodies, the four edges stretched out above, and two edges from each touched one of the creatures. Their legs were straight, and their feet were hoof-like and metallic.

There was bright light both around and between the creatures, with rapid flashes of light. Spread out above their heads was what looked something like a vault, sparkling like crystal, and awesome.

Then a fifth object appeared above the four: it looked like a throne made of sapphire. High above, on the throne was a human figure.

From his waist up he looked like glowing metal, as if full of fire, and from there down he looked like fire; and brilliant light surrounded him. Like the appearance of a rainbow in the clouds on a rainy day, so was the radiance around him. This was the appearance of the likeness of the glory of Yahweh.

"When I saw it, I fell facedown, and there came a voice from above the vault over their heads as they stood with lowered wings, and I heard the voice of one speaking.

(The description now includes a lengthy message from the voice.) *...Then the Spirit lifted me up, and I heard behind me a loud rumbling sound as the glory of the Lord rose from the place where it was standing. It was the sound of the wings of the living creatures brushing against each other and the sound of the round objects with them, a loud rumbling sound. The Spirit then lifted me up and took me away, and I went in bitterness and in the anger of my spirit, with the strong hand of the Lord on me.*

I came to the exiles who lived at Tel Aviv near the Kebar River. And there, where they were living, I sat among them for seven days—deeply distressed.

Ezekiel's encounters did not end there. For many years after this first encounter, Ezekiel had dozens of recurring visitations. The entire book of Ezekiel is dedicated to such encounters. Almost all of them include a similar voice, giving Ezekiel a message of warning to deliver to the people. In some, the same round objects and creatures are described. In some only the shining man is described. In some, the voice seems to come to him from nowhere, with no visual descriptions included. In a few instances, it seems that Ezekiel is transported elsewhere. Those particular instances will be addressed in the chapter on the Fourth Kind.

A Mighty Wind

In the book of 1 Kings, chapter 19th, we read the story of Elijah witnessing a series of phenomena that appear to include a tornado, an earthquake, a fire, and a whisper. Elijah had recently fled into the desert to avoid highly politicized death threats, and after forty days eventually wound up in a cave on Mount Horeb.

It was here in the cave that the Hebrew text says that דְבַר־יְהוָה (debar Yahweh) came to him with a message. This phrase is translated "the word of Yahweh", or more often, mistranslated "the word of the lord". 'Debar' is used quite commonly throughout the Hebrew scriptures, and is often translated to the English word, 'word'. This meaning is not entirely accurate. A more accurate translation, in general, would be something like 'commands', 'law', or 'message'. Its meaning is also closely tied to the idea of causality, and it is often translated "because of"[40], "in the matter of"[41].

---

[40] Genesis 12:17, Genesis 20:11, Genesis 20:18, Genesis 43:18, Exodus 8:12, 1 Chronicles 10:13, Deuteronomy 23:4

[41] Exodus 22:9, Numbers 16:49, Numbers 18:7, Numbers 25:18, Numbers 31:16, Deuteronomy 15:2, Deuteronomy 17:9,

The original Hebrew text does not imply a voice or sound. The English translations (in every version in fact) falsely imply a vocal phenomenon. There is no evidence in the text for this, and this is another example of a very poor translation that has somehow avoided detection for hundreds of years, and slipped through the cracks to remain in every single English version of the Bible. It just isn't true. The voice of God is not mentioned in the original Hebrew passage. Rather a message came to Elijah, "because of Yahweh", or "in the manner of Yahweh". Elijah received a message, and he understood its source as being from his god, Yahweh. It is entirely possible that this message was delivered to Elijah telepathically.

This idea is intriguing, and may be bolstered further by even more layers of meaning inherent in the word 'debar'. Debar also implies action, rather than a passive message. In fact, in both Judges 19:24, and Deuteronomy 22:24, the word debar is translated as "the action of", rather than "the word of". Another possible translation exists though, for many examples exist where debar indicates an entirely different concept; that of 'portion', 'amount', or 'allotment'[42].

To fully understand what Elijah witnessed, it is necessary to allow the word 'debar' its full range of meaning. A message came to Elijah because of, and in the manner and the portion of, and by the action of Yahweh. This is the setup for the encounter. Now the details follow;

The Lord said, "Go out and stand on the mountain in the presence of the Lord, for the Lord is about to pass by."

Deuteronomy 19:4, 1 Kings 9:15, 1 Chronicles 26:32, 1 Chronicles 27:1, 2 Chronicles 19:11

[42] Exodus 5:13, Exodus 5:19, Exodus 16:4, Leviticus 23:37 1 Kings 10:25, 2 Kings 25:30, 2 Chronicles 9:24, 1 Kings 8:59

> *Then a great and powerful wind tore the mountains apart and shattered the rocks before the Lord, but the Lord was not in the wind. After the wind there was an earthquake, but the Lord was not in the earthquake. After the earthquake came a fire, but the Lord was not in the fire. And after the fire came a gentle whisper. When Elijah heard it, he pulled his cloak over his face and went out and stood at the mouth of the cave.*[43]

Elijah was confronted by a mighty wind upon the mountain; a great and powerful force that split the very rocks of the mountain, and which was immediately followed by a tremendous shuddering, as the mountain itself was shaken as in an earthquake. A fiery blast followed the shaking, and then it died out to a quiet lingering whisper, perhaps a hiss. The combination and particular order of these phenomena bear a striking similarity to the expected effects of a large spaceship landing atop the mountain.

It is now that Elijah exits the safety of the cave, careful to wrap his face in his cloak, and then he receives his message. At this point, the text does finally describe a voice, using the word קוֹל (qowl). Only after the loud, flaming shaking subsides, can the small voice be heard. For it is a close encounter indeed.

A Flying Scroll

The debar Yahweh later appears to another prophet, Zechariah.[44] In fact, Zechariah has several of these encounters. The first encounter Zechariah describes takes place in Babylon in the year 520 BC[45]. Unfortunately

---

[43] 1 Kings 19:11-13

[44] Zechariah 1:1

[45] Zechariah 1:1 - In the eighth month of the second year of Darius

Zechariah in describing his first encounter is focused strictly on the message he receives, and he does not give any other details. Three months later,[46] Zechariah has another encounter with the debar Yahweh. This one occurs at night, and he sees what he describes as a male entity on "a red horse" in the forest. There is very good reason to suspect that he uses the term 'horse' metaphorically. The one "horse" appears to be a vehicle of some kind for the humanoid being, but there are others who seem somewhat less horselike. The humanoid entity describes a team of independently mobile "horses" as *the ones Yahweh has sent to go throughout the earth.*[47] They seem to act as some kind of independently navigating scouting drones. They also have the ability to communicate back to their commander: *they reported to the messenger of Yahweh who stood among the myrtle trees, "We have gone throughout the earth and found the whole world at rest and in peace.*[48]

Zechariah continues describing weirder and weirder objects and entities with whom he engages in primarily political conversation. A lot of strange symbology is used, but a few things stand out, including a woman flying in a "lead basket"[49], two other women who flew with birdlike wings[50], and a ten meter long flying object in the shape of a tube that had been sent to decimate the city.

The Lord Almighty declares, 'I will send it out, and it will enter the house of the thief and the house of anyone who swears falsely by my name. It will remain in that house and destroy it completely, both its timbers and its stones.'[51]

---

[46] Zechariah 1:7 - On the twenty-fourth day of the eleventh month, the month of Shebat, in the second year of Darius
[47] Zechariah 1:10
[48] Zechariah 1:11
[49] Zechariah 5:5-8
[50] Zechariah 5:9
[51] Zechariah 5:4

A Fiery Mount

We have already briefly mentioned that Moses and his people spent forty years following a UFO around in the desert. The book of Exodus tells of their many hardships during this period. What would possess a man to dedicate so much time and energy to investigating a flying object? The answer may be found in Exodus 19:16-21.

On the morning of the third day there was thunder and lightning, with a thick cloud over the mountain, and a very loud trumpet blast. Everyone in the camp trembled. Then Moses led the people out of the camp to meet with the elohim, and they stood at the foot of the mountain. Mount Sinai was covered with smoke, because Yahweh descended on it in fire. The smoke billowed up from it like smoke from a furnace, and the whole mountain trembled violently. As the sound of the trumpet grew louder and louder, Moses spoke and the voice of the elohim answered him.

Yahweh descended to the top of Mount Sinai and called Moses to the top of the mountain. So Moses went up and Yahweh said to him, "Go down and warn the people so they do not force their way through to see Yahweh and many of them perish.

There are many striking similarities between this passage, and the story of Elijah's UFO encounter. Here again, there is an object descending from the sky. Again, it is incredibly noisy and violent, such that it shakes the mountain, and the people are warned to stay back a great distance for their safety.

It should be noted that this was not the first time that Moses or the people had witnessed this flying object. They had already seen it several days earlier, as revealed in Exodus 16:10.

While Aaron was speaking to the whole Israelite community, they looked toward the desert, and there was the glory of the Lord appearing in the cloud.

Here, witnessed by a crowd of thousands, the כָּבוֹד (kevod) of Yahweh appears. In fact, it was right after this that the Israelites were given the mysterious manna to eat. Not only did the entire nation witness this phenomenon, they literally owed their lives to it, depending on it for food. After such phenomenal experiences it is little wonder that Moses and his people desired to stay near the flying object as long as possible. Even so, they always remained careful not to approach too close. The pillar of fire and cloud remained in front of them, never directly above them. This is because they had to keep a reasonable distance. There is every reason to believe that the earth-shaking rumbling was ever-present along with the fire and smoke. The pillar remained in the distance as Moses was careful to protect the people from what may have been the burning outgassing or rockets or some other type of technological side-effects.

A Burning Bush

This rumbling fiery tower was not Moses' first UFO experience either. Several months before becoming the legendary saviour of Israel, he had what may have been his first encounter. And it was this encounter that altered the course of his life and sent him to Egypt to free his countrymen. This event is typically referred to as "the burning bush", but it turns out that this name may be a grave misinterpretation. Exodus chapter 3 tells the tale:

Now Moses was tending the flock of Jethro, his father-in-law, the priest of Midian. And he led the flock to the back of the desert, and came to Horeb, the mountain of the Elohim. And a messenger from Yahweh appeared to him in a flame of fire.

So far, this encounter sounds very similar to the other encounters of Moses. The primary elements are a fire and a mountain. It is interesting that the mountain seems to have already been known as "the mountain of the Elohim".

It seems that this particular mountain had a reputation for these types of encounters, due to the experiences of previous travelers in the area.

Now a strange word appears in the story - הַסְּנֶה (hasseneh). This is the word that becomes translated into English as "of a bush". You may wonder what is strange about that. There's nothing strange about a bush. That's completely true. There is nothing strange about a bush. Bushes are extremely commonplace, even in the desert regions in which our story takes place.

The reader may recall the story of Abraham finding the ram in the bushes, as described in Genesis 22:13. The word used here is בַּסְּבַךְ (bassebak). It also occurs in Isaiah 9:18, Psalm 74:5, and Isaiah 10:34. A different word for bushes, שִׂיחַ (siah) is used in Genesis 2:5, Genesis 21:15, and Job 30:4

The Hebrew language has not one, but two distinct words which mean bush. There is no ambiguity with either of these words. Their meaning is abundantly clear from the context of the passages in which they are used, and there are multiple instances which one may cross reference to validate the meanings.

Unfortunately, this is not the case for the word 'hasseneh'. There are only two spots in the bible where the word 'hasseneh' is used. One is this story of Moses encountering fire on the mountain of the Elohim, in Exodus 3. The only other occurrence appears in Deuteronomy 33, forty years later, as Moses is remembering this exact event. Every single instance of the word 'hasseneh' points to this fiery mountaintop experience. Moses chooses not to use the obvious words that mean bush, and instead chooses a very obscure word whose meaning may only be guessed at.

Contextually, there is no indication that Moses is looking at a bush. The context indicates quite the contrary in fact.

And he led the flock to the back of the desert, and came to Horeb, the mountain of the elohim. And a messenger from Yahweh appeared to him in a flame of fire (from the midst/from among) **the hasseneh**. *So he looked, and behold,* **the hasseneh** *was burning with fire, but* **the hasseneh** *was not consumed. Then Moses said, "I will now turn aside and see this great sight, why* **the hasseneh** *does not burn."*

The hasseneh is visible from a distance and appears to contain fire. The hasseneh is non-flammable and unaffected by the fire within it. The hasseneh contains not only fire, but a living entity, identified as the messenger of the elohim. A second entity is identified within the hasseneh. None other than Yahweh.

So when Yahweh saw that he turned aside to look, the elohim called to him from the midst of the hasseneh and said, "Moses, Moses!"

The elohim proceed to tell Moses not to come close. This harkens back to the pillar of fire once again. Even from this distance, Moses shields his face from the burning brightness.

With all of this, is there enough evidence to prove that Moses' encounter of Exodus 3 was definitely a UFO? Probably not, but one thing is sure. There is absolutely no evidence that it was a bush.

A Missing Ship

While on the subject of bushes, this may be a good time to examine the experience of Abraham and Isaac. There is not much evidence to suggest a UFO encounter in this particular story, but there is a relevant point to be made. In Genesis 22, Abraham's faith is tested by Yahweh. Will Abraham trust Yahweh enough to offer his son as a sacrifice? There is an interesting point here regarding interpretation and translation, and how stories tend to evolve. This story appears in two very strong but very contradictory cultural memories. The story is preserved in the Jewish Torah as well as in the Qur'an of Islam. But each tradition identifies a different son of Abraham as the one who was sacrificed. The Qur'an does not specifically name the son, but Islamic tradition holds that it was Abraham's first-born son, Ismael. The Jewish/Christian tradition disagrees, stating instead that Isaac was the son sacrificed. In both cases, this story has great significance in that it ties two genealogical branches back to the patriarch Abraham, who is seen as the father of both religions. This is an excellent example and reminder that we must be cautious about details, and about simply believing what we are told.

One cannot so quickly move on from Abraham however. Aside from the sacrifice of his son, the story of Abraham contains a number of episodes which, although easy to ignore individually, when taken together, amount to what might warrant consideration as relevant to this investigation.

Genesis chapter 12 introduces Abraham part way into his story, by using a pair of past perfect verbs. Verse 1 and verse 4 act as parenthetical frameworks for a message attributed to Yahweh. *The Lord **had said** to Abram, "Go from your country..." — So, Abram went, as the Lord **had told** him.*

This is somewhat unusual because the past perfect tense describes a completed activity in the past. It is used to emphasize that an action was already completed before another action took place. In other words, it's an effective way to refer to an action while skipping the narrative details of that action.

Genesis 12 is essentially focusing on a message, while glossing over the means by which the message was delivered. But why would a narrator choose to skip the pertinent supernatural and amazing method by which the message was delivered? Wouldn't such details add credence to the message? A few verses later another backhanded reference adds another tidbit of information. Verse 6 and 7 give details about various local landmarks and attributes, yet only vaguely, and again with past present tense, reveal (almost begrudgingly) that *Yahweh* **had** *appeared to him.*

What is going on here? Why are there only vague references to the fact that Yahweh appeared both visibly and audibly to Abraham and gave him a message that was to prove ultimately central to the overall theme and narrative of the Bible? From a storytelling perspective it makes no sense at all. It is tantamount to J. R. R. Tolkien beginning his epic story with "so Bilbo had this magic ring."

But perhaps that is precisely the point. In a way, that is essentially how "the Lord of the Rings" begins. Why? Because it is actually a continuation of the storyline from "The Hobbit". It assumes the reader is already familiar with that other book. Could it be that the writer of Genesis 12 was simply assuming the reader would have already read the story of Yahweh's appearance to Abraham? Could there be some lost manuscript hidden away in some cavern for centuries that has yet eluded archaeologists and theologians alike? It is not out of the realm of possibility. Presumably the reader is aware of the famous Dead Sea Scrolls which were discovered in 1946 after having lain buried and lost to history for nearly two thousand years. Around the same time a second but lesser known stash of ancient documents was discovered: the Nag Hammadi Library. Both of these document collections revealed ancient texts which at one time were considered sacred scriptures to one group or another of ancient Jewish or Christian groups. Had they not been lost, some of these documents may very well have found their way into the modern Bible. What other documents remain unfound? Could the lost origin story of Abraham still be out there somewhere? If such a lost volume is ever found, what details will it reveal to fill in this story of how God "had appeared" to Abraham. Will it contain similar imagery as the encounters of Moses and Ezekiel, with fire and thunderous engines and strange round flying objects with flashing lights? We may never know.

The Emerald Man

Chapter 10 of the book of Daniel is another example of a bible story which leaves out the details of the flying craft. The story begins as Daniel encounters an unearthly being who communicates with him telepathically. Just as Ezekiel did, Daniel is careful to record the date and location of his encounter. *In the third year of Cyrus king of Persia... On the twenty-fourth day of the first month, as I was standing on the bank of the great river, the Tigris.*

Daniel is shocked to see a strange humanoid figure. *I looked up and there before me was a man dressed in linen, with a belt of fine gold from Uphaz around his waist. His body was like beryl* (some versions say topaz), *his face like lightning, his eyes like flaming torches, his arms and legs like the gleam of burnished bronze, and his voice like the sound of a multitude.*

The Hebrew phrase here interpreted as 'a man' does not actually imply a human being. The words אֶחָד (ehad) meaning 'one', and אִישׁ (ish) meaning 'male' are more directly interpreted as "a single male creature" Genesis 7:2 uses the same word 'ish' to refer specifically to the male of all species of animals. It is simply incorrect to translate this as "man". However, the creature is apparently wearing clothing, including a belt, which strongly implies that it is bipedal as well as civilized. The creature is clothed in בַּדִּים (baddim), which is translated as linen, however, it is worth noting that the only times that this exact word are used in the bible are here, and when describing the being from Ezekiel's UFO encounter. It would seem that the clothing worn by these two creatures was similar to each other, but differed somewhat from the ordinary linen word by ordinary people mentioned throughout the rest of the bible.

The entire next phrase "with a belt of fine gold from Uphaz around his waist" is a rather difficult one to translate, due to the fact the all five of the words used are essentially hapax legomena[52] in their exact forms. Thankfully, each is similar enough to other known words to justify that the standard translation is most likely at least somewhat accurate, if less precise than we may assume. However, it could just as easily read "with a shiny unknown object strapped to him.". There is decidedly more precision in the next phrase though. His body is described as "gemlike", and specifically, the gem indicated is כְתַרְשִׁישׁ (ketarsis) which translates directly to "beryl" which may indicate a number of different gemstones, but particularly signified in ancient times, those gems with a blue or green hue, in other words, emeralds. Translations using Topaz instead are a falsification. This may be done purposefully to shift the creature's perceived color to a more believable yellow or brown tint. The fact is, this passage states that the creature is green. Green, and probably also glowing or sparkling, as gemstones are wont to do.

Now the passage becomes even stranger. We are told his face looked like lightning and his eyes like torches. The word וּפָנָיו (upanaw) used here for face, appears to be closely related to a common word 'lepanaw' whose meaning is usually translated as "before" in the sense of placement, not in a timing sense, eg. "I came before the king, and a meal was placed before me". In other words, the phrase "in front of me" is a strong synonym. So, rather than his face looking like lightning, it may be more accurate to say that in front of him appeared to be a lightning-like effect.

---

[52] see Appendix D

The creature's eyes, וְעֵינָיו (wa-enaw) may mean eyes, or may just as easily refer to his vision or gaze. So this phrase could be interpreted as "his eyes burned like torches", which would seem to the modern mind to conjure some odd imagery of a laser-eyed super-villain, or perhaps it might mean "his vision glowed like a fiery torch", which sounds a lot more like some form of holographic image. In either case, it is a rather strange phenomenon to witness in the year 537 BC[53], thousands of years before the invention of either holograms or lasers. Daniel continues: *his arms and legs like the gleam of burnished bronze, and his voice like the sound of a multitude.* Gleaming metallic or metal-clad limbs and a voice modulator do nothing to detract from the overall disturbing effect of this strange visitor.

Next, Daniel confides that although he witnessed this creature with his own eyes, he was the only one to see it clearly.

I, Daniel, was the only one who saw the vision; those who were with me did not see it, but such terror overwhelmed them that they fled and hid themselves.

This appears somewhat self-contradictory. If Daniel's companions did not see anything, perhaps this was all in Daniel's mind or imagination. Yet, they were terrified, and fled, so they must have noticed something strange. Daniel continues:

So I was left alone, gazing at this great vision; I had no strength left, my face turned deathly pale and I was helpless. Then I heard him speaking.

Daniel has seen something that no-one else can see, and then he hears it speak to him. There appears to be at least some element of telepathic communication at play. If the creature had simply appeared and spoken verbally, the people with Daniel would have also seen and heard the

---

[53] Cyrus The Great's reign of the First Persian Empire is highly documented with well defined dates.

same things, but he makes a point of telling us that they did not. Is it possible that Daniel's companions fled, not due to the phenomena itself, but rather, because of Daniel's reaction to it? Daniel has basically just become deathly pale and collapsed on the ground. But that isn't really something that would make a crowd scatter in terror.

To rectify this contradiction, it may be presumed that the crowd was aware of some kind of phenomenon taking place. None of them got a good look at the visitor, but perhaps they ran away at the sight and sound of his spaceship landing. We don't know. Daniel doesn't mention any of that. Another interpretation would be that the crowd saw and heard some of the same things Daniel describes, but they received this information with much less clarity than did Daniel. This may be due to Daniel's already established reputation and proclivity with supernatural phenomena.

The Esteemed

We are given an intriguing clue in the body of the message that the being gives to Daniel.

*As I listened to him, I fell into a deep sleep, my face to the ground. A hand touched me and set me trembling on my hands and knees. He said, "**Daniel, you who are highly esteemed,** consider carefully the words I am about to speak to you, and stand up, for I have now been sent to you." And when he said this to me, I stood up trembling.*

Firstly, it is notable that the alien being knows Daniel's name! He calls him by name and by reputation: "you who are highly esteemed." Esteemed by whom? Why does this creature address Daniel this way?

Daniel was highly esteemed to be sure — both by men and by whoever sent this messenger. Daniel's career had begun thirty years previous in 587 BC, as a captive foreign courtly intern of sorts, under King Nebuchadnezzar.

He quickly made a name for himself as a skilled dream interpreter and prophet, rising within the next twenty-five years[54] to the rank of High Priest and Chief of the Magicians[55], reporting directly to the king. In 550 BC, under the rule of Belshazzar, Daniel was employed by the court in a senior position.[56] By the time the encounter of Daniel 10 took place in 537 BC[57] Daniel's seniority and reputation are well ingrained. A further clue comes fifteen years later, in 522 BC;[58] Daniel, now an old man, has another encounter which seems to relate. Daniel chapter 9[59] tells the tale:

Gabriel, the man I had seen in the earlier vision, came to me in swift flight about the time of the evening sacrifice. He instructed me and said to me, "Daniel, I have now come to give you insight and understanding. As soon as you began to pray, a word went out, which I have come to tell you, for you are highly esteemed.[60]

The earlier vision mentioned here is that of Daniel chapter 8, where Gabriel is also mentioned by name. This Gabriel character does not seem to be the same person described as the emerald man.

This raises many questions but also gives a few answers. It seems to indicate that some otherworldly beings are listening to Daniel, despite the fact that on this occasion Daniel seems to be alone in his room, meditating quietly[61]

---

[54] Sometime before the end of Nebuchadnezzar's reign in 561 BC.

[55] Ken Goudsward, "Magic In The Bible", 2019, p 43

[56] Daniel 8:1, Daniel 8:27

[57] the third year of Cyrus of Persia

[58] in the first year of Darius, Daniel 9:1

[59] note that the chapters of Daniel are not in chronological order. Chapter 9 takes place fifteen years after Chapter 10

[60] Daniel 9:21-23

[61] see Daniel 9:3, Daniel 9:20

These beings are numerous and have their own internal communication system enabling "a word" to "go out". These beings have some type of ability or technology to enable "swift flight". By now, Daniel somehow knows "the man" by name, calling him Gabriel, and recognizes that he has seen him before.

So, in summary, an emerald-skinned humanoid wearing strange clothing and equipment appears to deliver a message to a famous psychic, leaving a crowd of terrified onlookers in his wake, who may or may not have seen him arrive in a UFO. Aside from this incident, Daniel is also visited on at least two occasions by a flying psionic character named Gabriel, whose physique is not unusual enough to merit description and who possibly represents a different group from the emerald skinned fellow, but both groups are aware of Daniel's reputation.

The Watchers

If Daniel was worthy of such esteem and inter-elohim discussion and planning, one must wonder if he was an isolated case, or if other humans were watched with such care. Our attention turns once again to Moses. As already noted:

The Elohim called to him from within the bush, **"Moses! Moses!"** *and Yahweh said,* **"I have indeed seen** *the misery of my people in Egypt.* **I have heard them** *crying out because of their slave drivers, and I am concerned about their suffering. So I have come down to rescue them ... So now, go.* **I am sending you** *to Pharaoh to bring my people the Israelites out of Egypt."*[62]

The Elohim have seen and heard what has been happening in Egypt and elsewhere, and they know Moses by name. The Elohim are watching earth. They are

---

[62] Exodus 3:4-10

watchers. This term watchers is used three times in Daniel chapter 4[63], but the Bible does not give details about them. The watchers, do however, play a prominent role in the complex tale of the Nephilim and the fallen angels. It is a somewhat curious fact that the fallen angels tales are accepted without question into the greater Judeo-Christian mythos, even though their story is not contained in the Bible, whereas the watchers are far less accepted. The watchers are part of that same story. Neither group is part of the canonical Bible though, so that is all that can be said in the context of this book, which is limited to the Bible.[64]

The Sinai Hikes

Again our attention returns to Moses. Few Bible characters are as highly esteemed as he. Since Moses was esteemed among men and chosen by God, it makes some sense that he would be chosen to lead his people to freedom and blessed with certain special privileges. Yahweh calls Moses specifically by name, to come meet him on Mount Sinai, warning him that anyone else who approaches will surely die.[65]

"Moses alone is to approach the Lord; the others must not come near. And the people may not come up with him."[66]

It is a popular belief that Moses went up the mountain to receive the ten commandments from God. This is a major oversimplification. According to the book of

---

[63] Daniel 4:13, Daniel 4:17, Daniel 4:23

[64] The curious reader may investigate the Book of Enoch, 2 Enoch, the Book of Giants, Philo, Jubilees, and the Zohar, or check in on my webpage at ufo.dimensionfold.com

[65] Exodus 19:12, 21-24

[66] Exodus 24:2

Exodus, Moses hiked up and down Mount Sinai five, or possibly six times.[67]

His first two hikes are essentially to establish contact and safety protocols. Trip one and two are outlined in Exodus 19:1-14. Trip three occurs three days after trip two,[68] and immediately following the fiery descent of Yahweh as has been discussed in a previous section.[69] It is unclear why this dramatic phenomenon is not mentioned during Moses' first two trips. Or is it?

As discussed in a previous section[70], a much smaller version of this phenomena has already been described. That of the 'hasseneh'[71]. The two events both include fire, verbal (or perhaps psychic) communication, and the need to stay far away from the object. The only real difference is the sound and violent trembling that occurs, as well as the quantity of fire and smoke generated. Could it be that trip one and two are initiated by the appearance of the 'hasseneh'? Is the hasseneh a smaller scale version of what Moses experienced on trip three? Whatever the case, day three holds an unmistakable appearance witnessed by all, after which Moses initiates a third trip. On this trip, Yahweh again reiterates the safety protocols, then sends Moses back down with instructions to have his brother Aaron join him on trip four.[72]

At this point the narrative breaks to a direct communication from Yahweh. He seems to be addressing the entire crowd, although it is not clear exactly how that is

---

[67] The discrepancy arises from trip four, which may have actually been two trips. This is discussed further in footnote 75 on the following page.

[68] Exodus 19:16

[69] A Fiery Mount, page 41

[70] A Burning Bush, page 42

[71] see page 43

[72] Exodus 19:20-25

accomplished. The communication includes the famous "Ten Commandments". Before Yahweh can finish his message to the crowd, panic breaks out, and a modified delivery method is chosen.

And all the people were watching and hearing the thunder and the lightning flashes, and the sound of the trumpet, and the mountain smoking; and when the people saw it all, they trembled and stood at a distance. Then they said to Moses, "Speak to us yourself and we will listen; but do not have God speak to us, or we will die!" [...] So the people stood at a distance, while Moses approached the thick darkness where God was. Then the Lord said to Moses...

The next three chapters of Exodus contain the lengthy completion of Yahweh's message, delivered only to Moses. Moses then gives the crowd a verbal summary[73] before retiring by himself to write it down on paper.[74]

At this point, Yahweh modifies his guest list, telling Moses "*Come up to the Lord, you and Aaron, Nadab and Abihu, and seventy of the elders of Israel*" Thus begins Moses' fourth trip up the mountain.[75]

---

[73] Exodus 24:3

[74] Exodus 24:4

[75] A brief administrative interjection is required at this point. Although it may not be warranted by the text, an assumption is made here that the group of seventy-five descend the mountain at some point, and possibly Moses does too, before immediately ascending again. The confusion arises from two possibly conflicting facts. In Exodus 24:12-14, Moses and Joshua are called in to meet with Yahweh, and Moses tells the rest of the team to wait there (on the mountain), yet, before Moses descends, Aaron is present back in the camp. This will be discussed further in the *Golden Calf* section but is brought up at this point merely to delineate the fourth trip, from a possible fifth trip involving only Moses and Joshua.

The Seventy-Five

The safety protocols specified that only Moses could approach. Within three days, the rules changed, to allow Moses' brother Aaron to join him. Then, within hours, Joshua, Nadab and Abihu, and seventy elders are also allowed up the mountain. It makes one wonder if this is due to a sudden added availability of safety equipment or perhaps positive results from some kind of safety test. This will be explored more fully in a later section.

Moses received dire warnings that no one can ascend the mountain for fear of death. Later, in Exodus 33, God reiterates this same rule, telling Moses *"you cannot see my face, for no one may see me and live."*[76] Yet, the seventy five elders of Israel apparently *saw God, and they ate and drank.*[77] There appears to be some contradiction between these verses. Perhaps further analysis is required, focusing more deeply on the original Hebrew words.

For comparison, here is a full transcription of the New International Version for Exodus 24:9-11

*Moses and Aaron, Nadab and Abihu, and the seventy elders of Israel went up **and saw the God of Israel**. Under his feet was something like a pavement made of lapis lazuli, as bright blue as the sky. But God did not raise his hand against these leaders of the Israelites; **they saw God**, and they ate and drank.*

Does this translation accurately portray the Hebrew text? The primary question here is what did the elders see? Verses 10 and 11 both state that the elder saw God. In both of these verses the term used is elohim, rather than Yahweh.

Previously in this book, under the heading *Two Camps*[78], we briefly discussed the elohim. Elohim is a

---

[76] Exodus 33:20
[77] Exodus 24:11
[78] see page 10

plural word. It is a descriptive word. It is most definitely not a proper name. It does not refer to a particular character. The elohim are a sentient non-human race. Jacob was very clear that these beings are different. Yet, they are physical beings, rather than some kind of ethereal or spiritual concept. They slept in a camp. They could be engaged in wrestling matches.

Yahweh is not the same as elohim. The words are different. Yahweh is a proper name. Yahweh is a single character, rather than a group of beings. Deuteronomy 6:4 reveals that Yahweh is one of the elohim. Typically, this fact is obfuscated by poor translation. *Hear, O Israel: The Lord our God, the Lord is one.* This is a terribly misleading translation. The Hebrew text actually reads as follows:

שְׁמַע יִשְׂרָאֵל יְהוָה אֱלֹהֵינוּ יְהוָה ׀ אֶחָד׃

Transliterated for pronunciation, this is: *Sema Israel! Yahweh elohenu, Yahweh ehad!* One can almost begin to instinctively pick up the meaning, simply due to the presence of a few familiar words. The direct meaning should be blatantly obvious to even the most novice translator: *Hear Israel! Yahweh of the elohim, Yahweh is the one!*

This single verse gives a clear distinction between the words Yahweh and elohim, and even gives a succinct description of the relationship between the elohim, Yahweh, and the people of Israel.

- Yahweh is one of the elohim.
- The elohim includes, but is not limited to Yahweh.
- Yahweh is simply the elohim that is correlated to Israel.

Translating both words 'Yahweh' and 'elohim' into the same word 'God', results in huge discrepancies from the original Hebrew text, and huge problems with interpretation. Many ostensible contradictions in the Bible can be resolved by recognizing that the word 'God' has become essentially meaningless. We cannot differentiate between two very different meanings that this word has come to be used for. This is certainly the case in the book of Exodus. When Exodus 33 states *no one may see me and live*, this is Yahweh speaking. No one can see Yahweh and live. When the seventy-five elders saw God, they did not see Yahweh. Exodus chapter 24 uses the word elohim in both verses 10 and 11. The word Yahweh does not appear in this section of the story. So, have we skirted the issue of the apparent contradiction? Unfortunately, no. Verse 10 uses the word elohim, but it does so in conjunction with the word Israel. God is referred to here as "the elohim of Israel", which, according to Deuteronomy 6:4 is Yahweh. It seems we are left with the same problem. The seventy-five elders are precluded from seeing God by Exodus 33, yet here they are on Mount Sinai, gazing upon God. How can this be? Let us continue to step through this passage word by word.

Moses and Aaron, Nadab and Abihu, and the seventy elders of Israel went up and saw the God of Israel.[79] They saw the "elohim of Israel" (whom we now know to be Yahweh). The word for 'saw' is וַיִּרְאוּ (wayyiru). This word is used numerous times throughout the Bible and it is clear that the meaning is 'saw'. However, it is only one of several words that also mean 'saw', just as in English, we have numerous words with almost the same meaning, such as 'looked', 'noticed', 'gazed', 'spotted', 'stared', etc.

The usage of 'wayyiru' is not a simple "look" or "see". It has some heavy connotations. Wayyiru is generally used only in two specific contexts; it is either a "conspiratorial desire"[80], or a "stunning realization"[81], rather than a simple 'looking'. Certainly, this second meaning seems to fit this particular case, as seeing God

---

[79] Exodus 24:9-10
[80] Genesis 6:2, Genesis 12:14, Genesis 37:18, Genesis 37:25
[81] Genesis 37:4, Genesis 42:35, Exodus 5:19

would obviously be a stunning realization. The seventy-five elders have witnessed their lord, the elohim of Israel. Of course they are experiencing some shock and awe. What is strange about this is the next phrase. Rather than dwelling upon the glory of the most high and worshipping him as could be expected, they appear to be distracted by the flooring.

Under his feet was something like a pavement made of lapis lazuli, as bright blue as the sky. Could this be right? Is this really what the seventy-five elders, the leaders and wise men of the nation, are choosing to focus on? Perhaps there is a translation problem here. The phrase 'under his feet' consists of two words, וְתַחַת (wetahat), and רַגְלָיו (raglaw). 'Wetahat' is an interesting word with a couple of different meanings. Approximately half the time it seems to mean 'under', however, the other half of the occurrences, this word is translated as 'instead'[82]. 'Raglaw' is slightly less versatile. In general, the usage does indicate the feet or legs of a person. However, it is also used somewhat metaphorically, in the same way that English speakers may refer to the legs of a table or the feet of a chair. In this context, we may also use the word 'base' or 'stand'. Additionally, several instances of 'raglaw' seem to imply 'endurance'[83]

The next word is כְּמַעֲשֵׂה (kema-aseh). This word refers to works of fine craftsmanship and the actions such objects perform. In Leviticus 18:3, 'kema-aseh' indicates the man-made technological systems of politics, economics, and religions of Egypt and Canaan. Elsewhere it refers to metalworking[84] and engineering[85]. The English word that best matches this would be "machine". The next

---

[82] Job 31:40, Proverbs 21:18, Isaiah 3:24, Isaiah 60:17
[83] https://biblehub.com/hebrew/raglav_7272.htm
[84] 2 Chronicles 4:5, 1 Kings 7:26
[85] 1 Kings 7:33

word is לִבְנַת (libnat) which is a variation of a word which occurs only twice in the Bible[86] In both cases it is translated as Poplar, a type of wood. There is absolutely no rationale for the English word 'paved'.

The next word הַסַּפִּיר (sappir) is literally sapphire. There is no doubt on this one. The word is pronounced almost the same and is unmistakable across dozens of languages, having been borrowed through the centuries into many language groups.

To complete the verse, the next three words work together as an adjective phrase; וּכְעֶצֶם (uke-esem) הַשָּׁמַיִם (hassamayim) לָטֹהַר: (latohar). The typical translation here is *as bright blue as the sky*. This translation completely ignores some important connections and implications. 'Hassamayim' is used both for sky and for space. When God created the heavens and the earth, and the "great lights" in the sky, this same word is used. It is the home of birds and angels. In either of these uses, this word is a vast and spacious openness. It is a realm where action occurs. It has structure, albeit an invisible one. Contrary to many medieval and renaissance paintings, the Bible does not render the sky as a one-dimensional lifeless backdrop against which the shadows or reality are cast. 'Uke-esem' adds to this feeling. Though not a direct translation, the word 'uke-esem' is closely associated with 'bones'. Again, a sense of buried structural components is being conveyed, almost subliminal. On top of this, 'latohar' is added. 'Latohar' means clarity. Another translation reads *it was very like the heavens in its clarity*.

So where does all this analysis take us? *Gazing with stunning realization upon the 'god of Israel', instead endured a machine of wood and sapphire. It was a precise depiction of the structure of the heavens, clear and*

---

[86] in Genesis 30:37 and Hosea 4:13

wonderful. Suddenly, a sense of clarity descends upon the whole scene.

"Instead" (wetahat) is the key word to resolving this apparent contradiction. *Instead* of the actual Yahweh, the elders were gazing upon a contraption clad with wood and sapphire which *depicted* two things: it depicted a mathematically precise cosmic structural model, and above this, an animated image of Yahweh. Thus, there would be no repercussions for "seeing God". *God did not raise his hand against these leaders of the Israelites; they saw God, and they ate and drank.*[87]

This also solves an apparent discrepancy in the following verse. The next thing that happens is that Yahweh himself calls Moses up to a private area to meet with him personally. This takes place in Exodus 24:12 and will be discussed in greater detail in a subsequent section. Suffice to say for now, the traditional reading doesn't make sense. If Moses is already eating with Yahweh, how can Yahweh call him to come to where he is? Yahweh is not in fact in person, eating with the elders. He appears there via some kind of remote telepresence, streaming in from his private quarters.

Overall, the entire chapter makes a lot more sense under such an interpretation. The scene is one of enlightenment, humility, and unity. The elders and the elohim seem to be feasting in a large ship, big enough to hold dinner for at least seventy-five. Depending on your interpretation, it may feature a stunning computerized display of the cosmos, or simply a really really nice blue floor. In any case, it sounds like a nice place. It most certainly is not simply some tent on a rocky mountain slope. Not only that, but the ship has accommodations for staying overnight and longer. Moses and Joshua stayed on board

---

[87] Exodus 24:11

for forty days[88]. It is a large vessel, built with living quarters and computerized navigation systems with a really great graphical user interface, easily understood at some level by even the most novice of observers who lacked the technical vocabulary to do it justice when they later wrote about it.

The Bard

When confronted by astounding technology from the future or from a highly advanced civilization, how can one adequately describe the wonders they have witnessed? Some witnesses are flabbergasted and speechless. Some gloss over details. Some are more eloquent.

The Israelite king David was one of the finest poets and most popular musicians the world has ever known. Although his melodies are lost to time, his lyrics are still being remixed and sung in churches and on radio to this day. The biblical book of Psalms contains no less than one hundred and fifty of his poems and songs. Some of his works also appear in other books of the bible, within the context in which they were written.

One such example is a song that is sometimes known as "David's Song of Deliverance". David wrote and performed this song in triumphant response to a recent series of battles in which his army defeated the Philistines. The story and song are found in 2 Samuel chapter 21 and 22 (the song is also included as Psalm 18).

A brief summary of the events of chapter 21 is as follows: Israel had been engaged in a long series of battles against a neighboring country, Philistia. Interestingly, the Philistine army included at least five giants. They are identified as four 'descendants of Rapha'[89] and a 'Gittite'[90]

---

[88] Exodus 24:18
[89] 2 Samuel 16, 18, 20, 22
[90] 2 Samuel 19

(brother of the famous Goliath who had been killed by David many years earlier).[91] The text of chapter 21 indicates that these giants, and the other Philistine warriors were killed in battle by David's soldiers (who are listed by name), using ordinary weapons including spears and swords.

Yet David's lyrics seem to indicate something other than a regular battle with regular weapons. Rather, he indicates a giant, noisy, flying object, not unlike that the one described by Moses and Ezekiel:

> *"In my distress **I called** to Yahweh;*
> *I called out to my elohim.*
> *From his temple **he heard** my voice;*
> *my cry came to his ears.*
> *He parted the heavens and **came down**;*
> *dark clouds were under his feet.*
> *He mounted the cherubim and **flew**;*
> *he soared on the wings of the wind.*
> *He made darkness his canopy around him—*
> *the dark rain clouds of the sky.*
> *Out of the brightness of his presence*
> ***bolts of lightning** blazed forth.*
> *The **earth trembled** and quaked,*
> *the foundations of the heavens shook;*
> *they trembled because he was angry.*
> ***Smoke rose** from his nostrils;*
> *consuming **fire came from his mouth**,*
> *burning coals blazed out of it.*
> *Yahweh **thundered from heaven**;*
> *the voice of the Most High resounded.*
> ***He shot his arrows** and scattered the enemy,*
> *with **great bolts of lightning** he routed them.*[92]

---

[91] 1 Samuel 17
[92] Psalm 18:6-14

Is David describing a UFO? Well, it was certainly a flying object, but it was not unidentified, for David clearly states the name: Yahweh Elohay (יְהוָֹה אֱלֹהָי), meaning 'Yahweh my elohim'. David knew what he was seeing. He describes Yahweh the same way that Moses and Ezekiel did: a very loud machine that splits the sky and descends to earth amidst much smoke and fire and flashing light. This sounds like some type of spaceship.

What is interesting here is the interactions mentioned. The ship shoots what appears to David to be some kind of 'lightning arrow', yet rather than decimating the enemy, 'his arrows' merely 'scatter' and 'rout' them. In other words, the spaceship is not opening fire with a deadly weapon (which would quite likely kill the soldiers of both armies), but rather, employing scare tactics to drive the enemy into chaos, allowing the humans on the ground, David's own army, to do the actual fighting and killing. The Israelite army was not forced into panic mode because they knew this ally was coming and would not harm them. This fact is evidenced by the opening stanza; David called to Yahweh, and Yahweh heard him and came down. It was a planned defensive maneuver on the part of David and his army. David tells us this in the lyrics:

> *"He reached down from on high and took hold of me;*
>> *he drew me out of deep waters.*
>
> *He rescued me from my powerful enemy,*
>> *from my foes, who were too strong for me.*
>
> *They confronted me in the day of my disaster,*
>> *but the Lord was my support.*
>
> *He brought me out into a spacious place;*
>> *he rescued me because he delighted in me.*
>> *the Lord turns my darkness into light.*
>
> *With your help I can advance against a troop;*
>> *with my God I can scale a wall.*

The spaceship was not there to win the battle offensively, but rather to provide a safe vantage point for David. The king and his men had previously planned this tactic, as outlined in chapter 21, verse 15-17.

Once again there was a battle between the Philistines and Israel. David went down with his men to fight against the Philistines, and he became exhausted. And (one of the giants) ...said he would kill David. But Abishai (...) came to David's rescue, struck the Philistine down and killed him. **Then David's men swore to him, saying, "Never again will you go out with us to battle, so that the lamp of Israel will not be extinguished."**

David and his army had arranged for David to stay safely away from the fighting, in order to protect his life, and the stability of the country. So David calls the ship using some kind of communication system, the ship comes down and 'beams him aboard'. We see this in David's description of how *"He reached down from on high and took hold of me"*, *"the Lord was my support"*, *"He brought me out into a spacious place"*

David even goes so far as to describe the manner in which he is taken aboard the ship; in some kind of glowing antigravity energy beam: *"the Lord turns my darkness into light."*, and *"with my God I can scale a wall."*

Nor is this the only instance of this scenario in the psalms of David. This concept of the ship waiting and watching above the clouds appears in several of his other pieces:
- Psalm 33:13-14 *The Lord looks down from heaven; he sees all the children of man; from where he sits enthroned he looks out on all the inhabitants of the earth*
- Psalm 102 *Hear my prayer, Lord, let my cry for help come to you. Do not hide your face from me when I am in distress. Turn your ear to me when I call,*

answer me quickly... he looked down from his holy height; from heaven the Lord looked at the earth

And again, there is the motif of the flying object that scatters the enemy. Psalm 68:1 *May God arise, may his enemies be scattered; may his foes flee before him.* Interestingly, in this song David uses the plural term 'elohim' rather than 'Yahweh', so his lyrics are actually *"let the gods arise and scatter their enemies"*. He goes on to sing of *"the elohim in their holy dwelling, father of the fatherless and a judge for the widows, who makes the solitary to dwell in a house"*

David states that when the elohim went out before the people in the desert and caused the earth to shake and the rain to fall.[93] One can picture a massive flying object, so huge that its tremendous sound rattles the ground and causes the atmosphere to cool and condense, resulting in rain showers or, as we have seen elsewhere, even thunder and lightning. David even mentions a freak snowfall in the desert.[94]

The flying ship is mighty and ancient, says David: *He who rides upon the highest heavens, which are from ancient times; Behold, He speaks with His voice, a mighty voice. And His strength is in the skies. Elohim, You are awesome from your sanctuary.*[95] He even details the ship having *the wings of a dove covered with silver, and tipped with glistening gold.*

Perhaps a stranger element of David's descriptions are the vast numbers of these flying ships that he attests to.

---

[93] Psalm 68:7-8
[94] Psalm 68:14
[95] Psalm 68:33-35

Psalm 68 states *"The chariots of the elohim are myriads, thousands upon thousands; Yahweh is among them. Zion is now in the sanctuary."*[96]

David describes not a single ship piloted by his monotheistic God, but rather, an uncountable number of ships, surrounding mount Zion on all sides, with Yahweh among the throngs of the elohim.

Architecture And Artifacts

Close encounters of the third kind, by definition, involve humans communicating with unearthly intelligent beings. This has been demonstrated to have occurred numerous times within the biblical texts. Thus far, little attention has been given to the type of communication occurring. That is, the form and content of the communications. In terms of content, patterns emerge to reveal that the type of messages received by the witnesses tend to be either instructional, or admonishing. The latter are typically couched in moral, ethical, and political agendas which to be frank, this author would prefer to avoid. The former, however, are both eminently germane to the topic and infinitely more interesting, due primarily to the type of instructional content. Certainly, there are plenty of instances of pure moral instruction, but what may be more fascinating is the sheer volume of architectural and engineering information given. Many of the biblical UFO encounters have a strong focus on providing detailed blueprints and construction plans. These information downloads are not simply textual, philosophical, metaphorical, or mythological. The information was received, and immediately triggered intense planning, coordinating, and activity on the part of the individual, or in most cases, a large group of individuals. These plans

---

[96] Psalm 68:17

were actually followed and the objects in question were actually built according to the specifications. Many of these objects became key central aspects of the Jewish religion, governance, and social structure. Our attention now turns to one of the most important of these—the Tabernacle.

The Tabernacle

Yahweh said to Moses, "Tell the Israelites to bring me an offering. You are to receive the offering for me from everyone whose heart prompts them to give. These are the offerings you are to receive from them: gold, silver and bronze; blue, purple and scarlet yarn and fine linen; goat hair; ram skins dyed red and another type of durable leather; acacia wood; olive oil for the light; spices for the anointing oil and for the fragrant incense; and onyx stones and other gems to be mounted on the ephod and breastpiece. Then have them make a sanctuary for me, and I will dwell among them. Make this tabernacle and all its furnishings exactly like the pattern I will show you."[97]

This information is part of a large download given to Moses, during his fifth trip (and forty day stay) in the UFO atop Mount Sinai. It includes detailed materials lists and build instructions for numerous articles of furniture[98], ceremonial items and other equipment, as well as for the building itself, which is to be called "the Tabernacle". The Ark of the Covenant is one of the items outlined in this passage—this fascinating piece merits its own section and will be discussed in detail in a later section.

The instructions for the Tabernacle and its components are very detailed and lengthy, consuming no less than six chapters of the Bible.[99] Exact sizes are given

---

[97] Exodus 25:1-9
[98] a table, a lampstand, etc. See Exodus 25:23-40
[99] Exodus 25-31

for all the dimensions of the building, which is essentially a large courtyard and tent. Why? What purpose does this exacting precision hold? What difference would it make to Yahweh, if Moses built a tent fifty feet long instead of forty-five feet?

Exodus chapter 26 goes into detail about particular types of draperies and wooden frameworks plated in gold, specifying the type of thread to use, how to design the various clasps, fasteners, and various other components.

One intriguing factor here is a discussion around the fabric for a very specific curtain. *"The curtain will separate the Holy Place from the Most Holy Place."*[100] Moses is specifically instructed to *"Make a curtain of blue, purple and scarlet yarn and finely twisted linen, with cherubim woven into it by a skilled worker."*[101] Typically, this verse is taken to mean that there are images of 'cherubim' embroidered onto or woven into the fabric of the curtain. Along with this, is the understanding that cherubim are a type of angel. So it is easy to picture a fancy curtain with lovely pictures of angels on it. However, there are a few major problems with this interpretation. The next several sections will outline specific problems with several aspects of this interpretation.

The Embroidery

In our examination of this curtain separating the Most Holy Place, it may be helpful to also consider a second curtain described by Yahweh just a few verses later: *"For the entrance to the tent, make a curtain of blue, purple and scarlet yarn and finely twisted linen—the work of an embroiderer."*[102] In this case, it is clear that the decorations

---

[100] Exodus 25:33
[101] Exodus 25:31
[102] Exodus 25:36

are an embroidered pattern. Notice that the actual image does not appear to be specified, at least not in this section of the text. Now, examine again the instructions for the first curtain. The word embroider is not used. Rather, the cherubim are to be "woven into it". It is not yet clear exactly what this might mean, but it is explicitly distinct from the act of embroidering used on the second curtain. Additionally, the second curtain is to be "contracted out" to a third party—some unnamed embroiderer. This is in stark contrast to the first curtain (and indeed, the rest of the structure and furnishings). This fact will be examined further in a moment.

The Graven Image

Recall that even before Moses' fourth trip up the mountain, the people had all agreed to the *Ten Commandments*, (which by the way, are the foundational pillars of Judea-Christian ethics and culture to this day, and not to be taken lightly). Out of these ten essential laws, one is extremely relevant here. *"Thou shalt not make any graven image, or any likeness of any thing that is in heaven above, or that is in the earth beneath, or that is in the water under earth"*.[103] Yahweh even makes a point of reiterating this particular command: *You shall not make other gods besides Me; gods of silver or gods of gold, you shall not make for yourselves.*[104]

So, did Yahweh really command Moses to go ahead and make a gold embroidered image of an angelic cherubim, a being who resides in heaven above or in the earth below? This interpretation seems extremely unlikely. Particularly, if one is to recall what happened to Aaron and his friends when they decided to ignore that law and make

---

[103] Exodus 20:4
[104] Exodus 20:23

a golden calf. Suffice it to say that all hell broke loose, resulting in capital punishment and death penalties for no less than three thousand of those involved in the incident.[105]

It seems rather safe to assume that Yahweh did *not* in fact command Moses to break his own law, by committing the sin of embroidering pictures of angels onto a curtain. What the bible actually says is that the curtain is to have *cherubim woven into it by a skilled worker.* Of course, this opens two further questions: "what exactly are cherubim?", and "just who is this skilled worker?"

The Specialist

The act of weaving cherubim into the curtain was something separate from an act of embroidery and was performed by a skilled worker of a different sort. In fact, Yahweh himself hand-picks one man to do the job. Yahweh trains him in the techniques required to follow the blueprints and carry out the construction. This is revealed in Exodus 31:

Now the Lord spoke to Moses, saying, "See, I have called by name Bezalel, the son of Uri, the son of Hur, of the tribe of Judah. And I have filled him with the spirit of the elohim in wisdom, in understanding, in knowledge, and in all kinds of craftsmanship, to create artistic designs for work in gold, in silver, and in bronze, and in the cutting of stones for settings, and in the carving of wood, so that he may work in all kinds of craftsmanship."[106]

Why would such special training be required for the construction of a simple tent? The Israelites were already living in tents. They already knew how to make them. They also already knew metallurgy and smithing. Remember that golden calf? Weaving and goldsmithing were not

---

[105] This story is found in Exodus 32
[106] Exodus 31:1-5

technologies that they would have needed to import, or even upgrade. So what exactly was it that Bezalel was taught by Yahweh? And why was such advanced knowledge a requirement for building the Tabernacle, and particularly this so-called curtain that was ostensibly just some fabric with a picture of an angel on it. An important clue exists in the verse above, but one would never know it by reading the verse in English. Once again, a terrible act of translation has been committed and allowed to continue by the modern biblical compilers. One phrase in particular bears further investigation:

I have filled him with the spirit of the elohim in wisdom, in understanding, in knowledge, and in all kinds of craftsmanship, to create artistic designs for work in gold, in silver, and in bronze.

Two issues will be examined here: the content of the instruction, and the method of instruction. First the content—we read that Bezalel was trained in:

all kinds of craftsmanship, to create artistic designs for work in gold, in silver, and in bronze.[107]

This translation is problematic. The word 'bronze' is the Hebrew word, וּבַנְּחֹשֶׁת: (ubannehoset), which is sometimes translated brass, or copper, but usually bronze. The reason for this exact translation is fairly sensible. This is because the stories told in the Bible are generally agreed up to a date range corresponding to the so-called 'bronze age' which is said to have followed the 'stone-age'. There is a good reason for this assumption. Around 3300 BCE, advances in metallurgy and kiln building techniques and a global trade network allowed the technology of bronze to spread world-wide. Bronze is an alloy of copper and tin, which is much tougher than either copper or tin by itself, and it is well suited for making weaponry and all types of utensils. At the time, iron was not in use, due to the fact that

---

[107] Exodus 31:4

the kilns of the era could not reach temperatures needed to melt iron. However, this does not mean that pure copper was never used. Just as with gold and silver, there were certain projects that were better suited to copper, than to bronze. The toughest alloy is not always the best material for the job. Even today, there are certain things that we chose copper for over steel or the many modern alloys available. Each metal has its own certain properties, some of which are preferred for various applications. Copper remains the standard metal preferred for applications requiring electrical conductivity. Gold is also an excellent electrical conductor, making it a good choice for projects without the typical budgetary constraints. But surely, the tabernacle doesn't have anything to do with electricity, does it?

There is another factor at play here. Within Jewish law there is a concept known as kil'ayim (כלאים) which means "mixture," or "diverse kinds". There are strict and detailed prohibitions which proscribe the planting of certain mixtures of seeds, grafting, the mixing of plants in vineyards, the crossbreeding of animals, the formation of a team in which different kinds of animals work together, and the mixing of wool with linen in garments. These laws are listed in Leviticus chapter 19, and Deuteronomy chapter 22. Although not specifically listed, it seems obvious that metallurgical alloys would be governed by the same type of standards. The objects listed in the Tabernacle build tend to be ceremonial or structural in nature. They are considered holy. It seems very likely that for such purposes, purity of material would be a far more desirable attribute than simple physical strength. Thus, copper, rather than bronze, seems to be a far superior choice of translation in this particular case.

Now that we have the materials sorted out, what exactly is it that Bezalel is supposed to do with these pure materials? The phrase *to create artistic designs* requires careful examination. It consists of three words in Hebrew, לַחְשֹׁב מַחֲשָׁבֹת לַעֲשׂוֹת, ("lahsob mahasabot la-asowet"). לַחְשֹׁב (lahsob) is a verb which can be translated as 'devise', 'plan', 'plot', 'calculate', or 'design'. It is used in many stories where the characters are laying out grand schemes. Likewise, the noun, מַחֲשָׁבֹת (mahasabot) has similar implications. It means 'thoughts', 'ways', 'purposes', 'plans', and 'plots'. So far, with just the first two words it seems that Bezalel was trained to 'design plans' or 'calculate purposes'

The third word here is another verb. It describes the noun (which has been identified as "plans or plots"). לַעֲשׂוֹת (la-asowet) means 'to do'. It is a generic action word. Sometimes, the translators use 'to perform'. Usually, a verb describes the actions of a subject. Here, the verb is describing the action of an object. That object is the plans or plots or schemes or purposes. The object is not a physical object. The object is the plan. The plan is described as being active.

So, Bezalel is taught to "design active plans" or "calculate active purposes". This language has a striking resonance to software engineering. As a computer programmer myself, I design and code programs to act autonomously. They are active plans whose purposes I have designed and calculated. I design active plans and I calculate active purposes. Is it possible that Bezalel, who was already skilled in fine craftsmanship and design, was receiving training in programming or computer operation? Is it possible that the architecture and artifacts within the Tabernacle are meant to function as some kind of computational device? Could this curtain have been some sort of *technological* component? Perhaps some kind of gold thread lattice or some kind of pattern that was integrated into the actual weave of the fabric itself. For what purpose? More information is required regarding this so-called 'cherubim'.

Before leaving this passage, however, some analysis is required with respect to the method of instruction given to Bezalel. Examining the passage again:

*I have called by name Bezalel, the son of Uri, the son of Hur, of the tribe of Judah. And **I have filled him with the spirit of the elohim** in wisdom, in understanding, in knowledge, and in all kinds of craftsmanship, to create artistic designs for work in gold, in silver, and in bronze, and in the cutting of stones for settings, and in the carving of wood, so that he may work in all kinds of craftsmanship.*

The bold section here comes from the Hebrew phrase, וָאֲמַלֵּא אֹתוֹ רוּחַ אֱלֹהִים (wa-amal-le otow ruach elohim). The classic translation is laden with modern post-trinitarian doctrine. "I have filled him with the spirit of the elohim." But again, the translation is shoddy. 'Wa-amal-le' means simply 'filled', or 'full'. 'Otow' is a very strange word. It occurs hundreds of times in the Bible but is never translated. Rather it seems to be used to affect or modify the sentence in some unknown way. In this case, the translation gives it the meaning 'him', but there is really no linguistic basis for the word 'him' appearing in this sentence. We do not truly know if the verb "full" is meant to refer to Bezalel himself, or if it refers to one of the other nouns in this sentence. The "wisdom" or the "understanding" are just as promising objects. The implication may just as well be that the curriculum, or the program, or the training material itself, was "full".

The Hebrew word רוּחַ (ruach) is a critical concept of theology. It is often translated 'spirit', as it is here, but its literal translation is 'breath', 'wind', 'mind', or 'mood'. The implications of 'ruach' are that of motivation, power, ability, and knowledge, and even aesthetic or style; similar to the way the word is still occasionally used in English phrases such as "the spirit of St. Louis", or the German word 'zeitgeist'. It does not necessarily imply the typical concept of an autonomous entity such as that which is personified in trinitarian doctrine. Perhaps one way to encompass many of these concepts in English would be with the phrase "the way of". This phrase bundles motivation, patterns, and style, which is truly what 'ruach' has to do. It is a powerful word with a lot tasked to it. So what this verse literally says is not "I have filled him with the Holy Spirit", but rather "full of the way of the elohim, Bezalel was trained".

Consider also Bezalel's name. Since he enters the narrative only after having received this instruction from the elohim, it is highly probable that his name has already been changed to reflect his new status. This practice is abundantly clear in the case of many other Biblical figures including 'Israel' meaning "contended with the elohim", and 'Abraham' meaning "father of many nations". Bezalel means "in the shadow of the elohim". His very name backs up the phrase "full of the way of elohim." He now inhabits their shadow.

So, what is the conclusion? Bezalel was filled in the way of the elohim, in wisdom understanding and knowledge and craftsmanship to design active plans or calculate active purposes in gold, silver, and copper. These are no mere architectural blueprints. The plans that Bezalel is working with are 'active'. Bezalel has been instructed in the technology of the elohim in order that he may create these active plans called the cherubim.

The Cherubim

At first blush, significant portions of the book of Exodus appear to be a set of instructions for a divinely inspired temple: the Tabernacle. As one examines the associated objects, however, a distinct impression begins to arise of something more than a simple static building. The instructions appear to indicate the development of something more mechanical, or perhaps, computational.

What exactly are these cherubim that Bezalel is supposed to work on? There are some clues buried in the book of Ezekiel. Ezekiel chapters 8-10 tells of another UFO encounter witnessed by Ezekiel. Again, he gives his precise location and the date. *In the sixth year, in the sixth month on the fifth day.*[108] Compare this to the date given in Ezekiel 1: *In my thirtieth year, in the fourth month on the fifth day.* Unfortunately, whereas Daniel gives dates based on the year of the reigning king, Ezekiel's dating methodology appears to be based upon his own life experiences. In the first case, it is clearly based upon his age— "in my thirtieth year". However, the second instance is clearly not a continuation of this method. "In the sixth year" he says. It is safe to assume that he is not referring to when he was six years old. The story references previous events earlier in the book, so we know that the book of Ezekiel is told in chronological order. Thus, when he says, "in the sixth year" it most likely means "six years later", and it appears to indicate that Ezekiel's second close encounter happened six years after his first.

This time, he does not witness the landing of the UFO. Rather, an alien entity enters his home *"while I was sitting in my house and the elders of Judah were sitting before me"*.[109] He describes "a fiery figure", "as bright as glowing metal." The being "stretched out what looked like a hand and took me by the hair of my head,", then "lifted [Ezekiel] up between earth and heaven [...] and took [Ezekiel] to Jerusalem.[110] At the time Ezekiel was living in Babylon as a forced immigrant or perhaps a prisoner of war, but not all the Jews had been captured by the Babylonian armies, and many remained in Jerusalem. After being teleported or transported via UFO to Jerusalem, Ezekiel

---

[108] Ezekiel 8:1
[109] Ibid.
[110] Ezekiel 8:3

witnesses some strange things[111], not the least of which is that of a spacecraft taking off. It appears to be the same craft he saw six years earlier. Ezekiel is now standing in Jerusalem, in the holy temple. *I looked, and I saw the likeness of a throne of lapis lazuli above the vault that was over the heads of the cherubim.*[112]

When he says "above the vault that was over the heads of the cherubim" he is referring to a physical location, in the temple. These cherubim are the decorations on top of the *Ark of the Covenant*. This ark was one of the items made by Bezalel for the Tabernacle, and it was eventually moved to the temple in Jerusalem, where it remained at Ezekiel's time. It is somewhat interesting that Ezekiel was allowed to see it, as the room containing it was considered sacred and only accessible to the high priests on special occasions. Nevertheless, this is what Ezekiel says happened.[113] Yahweh is here also, sitting upon the lapiz throne, and he sends one of his strange companions to fetch some "burning coals" or "fire" from between the cherubim below him, resulting in the whole room filling with smoke. Yahweh's ship then lifts off, moving out into the courtyard, with blinding light and a loud noise which Ezekiel refers to as the *sound of the wings of the cherubim*[114] Next, Ezekiel repeats the same scene in more detail. Yahweh's humanoid assistant (here called "the man in linen", and who according to Ezekiel chapter 9 seems to be some type of scribe and administrative assistant to Yahweh) is told *"Take fire from among the wheels, from among the cherubim" the man went in and stood beside a wheel. Then one of the cherubim*

---

[111] These events will be explored in a subsequent section.

[112] Ezekiel 10:1

[113] Ezekiel 8:16 *He then brought me into the inner court of the house of the Lord, and there at the entrance to the temple, between the portico and the altar...*

[114] Ezekiel 10:5

reached out his hand to the fire that was among them. He took up some of it and put it into the hands of the man in linen, who took it and went out. (Under the wings of the cherubim could be seen what looked like human hands.)[115]

So the scene is set up as the cherubim being ornamental decorations that are part of the Ark of the Covenant, but then they are described as having hands that are capable of interacting with the humanoid alien. Perhaps they are some sort of mechanism? Additionally, Ezekiel reveals the presence of wheels within or among these cherubim, despite the fact that wheels are not mentioned in the detailed plans for Bezalel to build the cherubim. Also, they are on fire. These fiery, noisy wheels are under the throne of Yahweh, which then lifts off noisily. Is this some kind of engine? Ezekiel continues: *I saw beside the cherubim four wheels, one beside each of the cherubim; the wheels sparkled like topaz.*[116] *[...] the four of them looked alike; each was like a wheel intersecting a wheel. As they moved, they would go in any one of the four directions the cherubim faced; the wheels did not turn about as the cherubim went. The cherubim went in whatever direction the head faced, without turning as they went. Their entire bodies, including their backs, their hands and their wings, were completely full of eyes, as were their four wheels. Each of the cherubim had four faces: One face was that of a cherub, the second the face of a human being, the third the face of a lion, and the fourth the face of an eagle. Then the cherubim rose upward. When the cherubim moved, the wheels beside them moved; and when the cherubim spread their wings to rise from the ground, the wheels did not leave their side. When the cherubim stood still, they also stood*

---

[115] Ezekiel 10:6-8

[116] A blue or green gemstone.

still; and when the cherubim rose, they rose with them, because the spirit of the living creatures was in them.[117]

Finally it dawns on Ezekiel: *These were the living creatures I had seen beneath the God of Israel by the Kebar River, and I realized that they were cherubim.*[118] How is it possible that Ezekiel doesn't recognize these so-called "living creatures"? Only after some detailed observation, he realizes their identity. How does he not notice this right off the bat? It's quite simple. When Ezekiel is transported to Jerusalem, he is taken into the holy sanctuary of the temple. Nobody is allowed in there, so apart from the rare visits by the high priest, no one has seen the Ark of the Covenant for hundreds of years.[119] Additionally, Jewish law forbids graphic arts. No pictures existed of the Ark of the Covenant. Be that as it may, Hebrew culture included a lot of educational material, particularly verbal education on religious topics, so every Hebrew kid from Jerusalem to Babylon would have known about the Ark of the Covenant and the cherubim adorning it. They would have heard many stories about it and would have been familiar with its history. They could probably even recite descriptions of its design that had been handed down since the days of Moses. They may even be the exact same descriptions we have, albeit he would have been reading them in the original language. But these descriptions were apparently woefully inadequate. Ezekiel had heard the descriptions. He knew the name. He knew the word 'cherubim' and the theoretical knowledge around it. But he had never *seen* it. Not even in a picture. He never put two and two together until he saw the Ark of the Covenant himself, with the actual "throne of god" spaceship hovering above it. He was standing there

---

[117] Ezekiel 10:9-17

[118] Ezekiel 10:15

[119] Ezekiel lived approximately 700 years after Moses and Bezalel and the creation of the Ark of the Covenant

staring at this revered artifact, and the parts on top which were designed to resemble or in some way replicate the real life version of the cherubim. He saw the spaceship hovering above them. He saw the resemblance of certain parts of the spaceship to the parts on the Ark of the Covenant. He saw their correspondence. Perhaps he saw their physical interaction. Only then could he recognize these parts of the spaceship as the thing he had been taught about all his life from a decidedly religious standpoint. He then could suddenly recognize that the weird spaceship thing bore a striking resemblance or correspondence to the cherubim. Only then could he recognize the cherubim for what they truly were—parts of an ancillary device that involved a docked spaceship. It is still not clear what role these cherubim play, but it becomes obvious to Ezekiel that the cherubim are *for* the spaceship. There is little other technical evidence to go on, but it is clear that the ship lands or docks over the cherubim. Perhaps they are part of a charging system or some kind of control unit. We just do not know. It is here that Ezekiel gets more technical data, including some technical jargon and the names of certain of these components. He had already known the term "cherubim", and now he gets the opportunity to learn some of the actual names of certain other parts which had not been included in his religious teaching: *I heard the wheels being called* הַגַּלְגַּל *(haggalgal).*[120] He overhears someone (perhaps the pilot and crew?) speaking about certain technological components as they prepare to launch. This is analogous to the type of chatter one would still hear before the launch of any aircraft.

"Engines ready?"

"Confirm, engines ready."

Then the glory of Yahweh departed from over the threshold of the temple and stopped above the cherubim.

---

[120] Ezekiel 10:13

While I watched, the cherubim spread their wings and rose from the ground, and as they went, the wheels went with them.[121]

Suddenly, I have more respect for the English translators of the Bible. They were in the same boat as Ezekiel. Or perhaps they were in the opposite boat. Ezekiel had a lot of experience with a technological object. He had seen this UFO not once but twice, plain as day, in broad daylight, from a very clear vantage point, and with plenty of time to take it in and really absorb what he was seeing. He had no language for it and had to try to make some kind of sense out of it, which he actually did a commendable job on. He described in great detail its appearance, its movements, and even, to the best he could figure out, how it worked. He just had no reason to think it was in any way related to his religious lessons. Why would he?

As for the English translators, up until the early 1500s, most translators didn't even have access to the Hebrew texts. They were essentially flying blind, with only Latin translations to work from. William Tyndale was able to get his hands on both Greek and Hebrew texts, and with the recent invention of the printing press, was able to produce and distribute a decent number of copies of the New Testament. Sadly, he was burnt at the stake for heresy before he could complete his Old Testament translation.

By 1611, the King James Bible was completed, by a team of several dozen translators, and was revised and standardized in 1769. All of this was done during a period that to the modern mind would certainly qualify as a veritable 'dark ages'. From a technological perspective, civilization was pretty much dead in the water. Industry consisted of men with hand tools. The steam engine had not yet become a widespread technology. Cars, electricity, modern machines, and computers would not even be

---

[121] Ezekiel 10:18-19

imagined for hundreds of years. Much less a spaceship. The European clergymen and government bureaucrats who produced the English Bible had plenty of experience in religious training. In this way they were similar to Ezekiel. But they had absolutely no framework for comprehending the mechanical nature of a flying ship made of gleaming metals shooting fire. In those days it was not possible to even make a building out of metal[122], much less something that could rise into the air.

One thing that was quite abundant however were ideas. Theoretical ideas. Mostly about philosophy and of course, religion. There were plenty of theories abounding about the nature of various and sundry ranks and forms of spiritual and ethereal beings. Some evil, some good. Some powerful, some not so much. Theorists loved to hypothesize regarding hierarchical rankings and roles and interactions. Thus, it is easy to see why, even when Ezekiel finally understands, his enlightenment did not make a big impact on the English translators. Quite frankly, they had no clue what he was talking about and when they tried to conceptualize it, they naturally fell into the thinking of the day, with its ranked spiritual beings. Sadly, they had no hope of even visualizing a graceful arcing shining hovering flashing mechanical object.

Regardless of their, or our own, ability or disability to comprehend, the Bible is abundantly clear that such flying objects do exist. Ezekiel saw one. Moses saw one. David saw thousands. These flying objects are inexorably tied to this concept of the cherubim, although we still can't say with any certainty what the cherubim actually are. In numerous Psalms, David refers to the fact that Yahweh seems to ride upon the cherubim: *He mounted the cherubim and flew; he soared on the wings of the wind.*[123] *You who*

---

[122] Architecture relied solely on stone, wood, and brick.
[123] Psalm 18:10

are enthroned above the cherubim, shine forth![124] The prophet Isaiah echoes this sentiment: *O Lord of hosts, the God of Israel, who is enthroned above the cherubim.*[125]

One may be left with the distinct feeling that perhaps the cherubim is just the name for the actual UFO itself. But that isn't the whole story. The very first appearance of the cherubim in the Bible gives a different impression altogether. All the way back in the opening chapters of Genesis, we find the cherubim:

And Yahweh of the elohim said, "The man has now become like one of us, knowing good and evil. He must not be allowed to reach out his hand and take also from the tree of life and eat, and live forever." So Yahweh of the elohim banished man from the Garden of Eden to work the ground from which he had been taken. After he drove the man out, he placed on the east side of the Garden of Eden **cherubim and a flaming sword flashing back and forth** *to guard the way to the tree of life.*[126]

In Genesis 3, to conclude the story of *Adam And Eve*, cherubim are placed to guard the entrance of Eden. But not only cherubim, "cherubim and a flaming sword flashing back and forth". This has a weirdly fantastical or even sci-fi ring to it. It sounds like some kind of automated patrol robot. Could the cherubim be the control box for the remote-controlled flaming sword? Of course, this is pure speculation, but if this were the case, it also makes sense why the cherubim are so closely associated with the "wheels" or engines and other components in the UFO. In both instances they seem to provide some kind of locational and spatial control.

The cherubim could be interpreted as some kind of robots, just as easily as some type of transdimensional

---

[124] Psalm 80:1
[125] Isaiah 37:16
[126] Genesis 3:22-24

spiritual beings, or even aliens. Is there enough new information to answer the question at hand? The question under pursuit is this—what were these cherubim that Bezalel was supposed to program? One must return to the design specifications listed in Exodus 25.

Make a כַּפֹּרֶת *(kapporet) of pure gold—two and a half cubits long and a cubit and a half wide. And make two cherubim out of hammered gold at the ends of the kapporet. Make one cherub on one end and the second cherub on the other; make the cherubim of one piece with the cover, at the two ends.*[127]

Firstly, a note is in order regarding the naming of this object. We have already seen a few instances where a novel technical term is given. Ezekiel learned the name of a few specialized components, including the cherubim, and the haggalgal. This is another case. Moses is being directed to oversee the building of a certain specific object called the 'kapporet'. This is a specific technical term given to Moses and Bezalel directly from Yahweh. There is no normal Hebrew word for it. It is a technical term which appears only in reference to this exact object. To call it anything else is purely misleading. Yet, attempts have been made to translate the name. Such names as "mercy seat" and "atonement cover" are typically applied, and in fact, these names may actually provide some useful information to the function of this strange object, as shall be expanded upon momentarily. We see, further that:

The cherubim are to have their wings spread upward, covering the kapporet with them. The cherubim are to face each other, looking toward the cover.[128]

There are several aspects here which are directly echoed in the UFO encounters of Ezekiel. Specifically, the words translated here as 'wings' and 'face'. We have

---

[127] Exodus 25:17-19

[128] Exodus 25:20

already examined how each of the cherubim is said to have had *"four faces and four wings."*[129] We then examined the Hebrew words פָּנִים (panim), and and כְּנָפַיִם (kenapayim) which we found they yielded a better translated as "four surfaces or edges". The same word 'panim' is also used in Genesis 1:2, where the ruach of elohim is said to hover over "the surface" (panim) of the deep.

Thanks to Ezekiel's second UFO encounter in Jerusalem, it is now clear that the cherubim have four surfaces. Suddenly, a geometric figure springs to mind—a solid object with four surfaces: a tetrahedron.

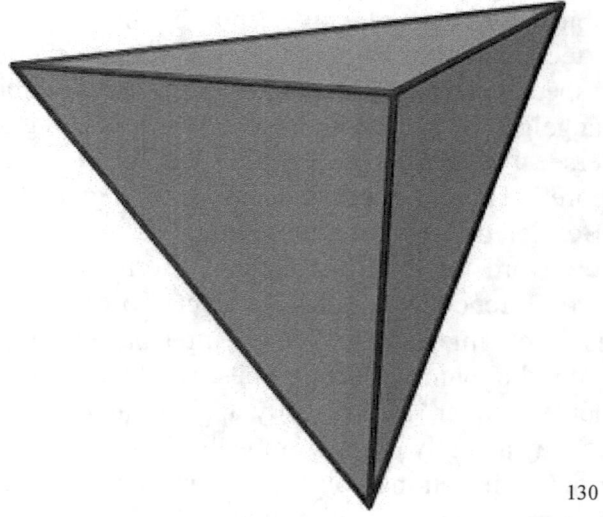

130

Six Wings

The figure above is said to be four sided, since it contains four surfaces. However, it could also be described

---

[129] Ezekiel 1:6, New International Version
[130] Image created by Cyp for Wikimedia and used under Creative Commons licence - CC BY-SA 3.0

as having six edges. The Hebrew word 'panim' is not exactly clear. It might mean 'surface' or 'edge'. The ruach of the Elohim may just as well have been hovering over the *edge* of the deep. This ambiguity is particularly interesting when we consider another UFO encounter. That of the prophet Isaiah. His description is very similar to certain aspects described by Ezekiel but differs in one regard: Whereas Ezekiel counts four "wings", Isaiah counts six.

In the year that King Uzziah died[131] *I saw the Lord sitting on a throne, high and lifted up, and the train of His robe filled the temple. Above it stood seraphim; each one had **six** wings [...] and the doorposts shook at his voice, and the house was filled with smoke.*[132]

Granted, Isaiah also gives these objects a different name, which is not terribly surprising, given the proclivity of names for such objects already. The שְׂרָפִים (seraphim) described by Isaiah may or may not be equivalent to the cherubim.[133] Suffice it to say that these objects, whether the same or not, are both seen to fly in close proximity with the "throne of Yahweh" and differ primarily in the number of edges or surfaces. This might be entirely due to the counting of geometric edges versus surfaces. Why does it matter? This brings us back to the book of Exodus, and back to yet another translation issue.

The cherubim are to have their surfaces spread upward, covering the kapporet with them. The cherubim are to face each other, looking toward the cover.[134]

Ostensibly, the wings, or edges, or surfaces are 'covering' the kapporet. This is a rather inaccurate

---

[131] In the year 740 BCE

[132] Isaiah 6:1-4

[133] An attempt to define the seraphim will be tackled as a separate project, for it is mainly tangential to this discussion. Look for an article from me on the web.

[134] Exodus 37:9

understanding. The word translated here as 'covering' is סֹכְכִים (sokekim) and the actually meaning is 'guardians'. It is not a verb, as is implied in the translation; rather it is clearly a male plural noun form, based on the verb 'to guard' and it can only, and unambiguously mean 'the guardians'. It is a title which is used only three times in the Bible, each time applied to these very cherubim that guard the kapporet.

In Ezekiel 28:14 the singular noun form of this word is applied to the guardian cherubim who stands with the flaming sword outside of Eden. Clearly, this cherubim is a guard. The word also appears in Nahum 2:5 where it typically gets translated to 'the defense'. It seems that there is more going on here than a simple covering. The surfaces of the cherubim appear to be intended to provide some kind of protection. What is somewhat less clear is whether they are meant to protect the kapporet, or to provide protection *from* the kapporet.

Recall that 'kapporet' is a technical term that refers only to this object. This object is designed to be placed on top of the Ark of the Covenant. Nicknames such as "mercy seat" and "atonement cover" have been applied to the kapporet. Perhaps the reason for such names is now becoming clear. The kapporet is a protective covering. It protects the high priest from whatever is inside the Ark. It truly is a mercy. It attones for the problem of coming close to the Ark. This is a serious problem indeed, as shall be detailed momentarily.

The Merkabah

A tetrahedron has been mentioned briefly, however, it requires further analysis. Consider the arrangement of the cherubim. There are to be two cherubim, and they are to face each other. In other words, they are facing opposite directions. Consider what geometrical wonders occur when two tetrahedrons are superimposed, facing opposite directions.

135

These two superimposed tetrahedrons now form a unique shape, and arguably the most important symbol in Hebrew history and culture. A couple hundred years after Ezekiel penned his book, Jewish scholars became increasingly interested in analyzing his account, eventually creating a large body of works focussing on the vehicle he described, which they began to refer to as the 'merkabah' (meaning 'chariot'). They recognized the object for what it is, a flying vehicle. The same vehicle that David describes in his psalms, with Yaweh travelling upon it. The Hebrew scholars developed a whole set of commentary and theology based around this object, as well as a rich

---

[135] Image created by Cass Reese for the Noun Project, used with permission

symbology. Their primary symbol continued to be this superposition of two tetrahedrons, shown sometimes from slightly differing angles, indicating a three-dimensional object that can be seen to rotate.

The rotation of the object was recognized as a critical feature. As already discussed in an earlier chapter, Ezekiel described the cherubim as "wheels within wheels" with flashes of lightning and fire. Combining this imagery with the three-dimensional, geometrical tetrahedral qualities of the merkabah traditions, we get a clearer picture that strongly resembles a gyroscope. This similarity is further enforced by Ezekiel's observation that they "do not turn as they move"[136] but only "move straight ahead" in any direction they choose. This is in fact the key feature of a gyroscope. A gyroscope is a device used for measuring or maintaining orientation and angular velocity, exactly as Ezekiel indicates. It is a critical piece of the navigation systems of modern helicopters, submarines, and space satellites. Could this explain the presence of such a device in Ezekiel's UFO encounter? Unfortunately, there is just not enough information to truly know the purpose of this device, which leaves the reader to speculate. Spinning components are used in all kinds of modern technology including electromagnetic generators and motors and they give rise to centrifugal and vortex forces. Could these or other as yet unknown forces and technologies be the real purpose of the wheels within wheels?

At any rate, there is no question that the merkabah symbology encapsulates great power. Unlike the majority of obscure ancient esoteric cults which have eventually waned and been lost to the faded memories of history, the merkabah lives on as a powerful symbol. Although it may be tempting to dismiss it as a fringe obsession, perhaps caution would be advised against such a cavalier attitude.

---

[136] Ezekiel 1:17

After all, only a very obvious graphical simplification is required to achieve the most obvious and intrinsic symbol of all of Judaism: one that will be immediately recognizable to every reader—the well-known Star of David, that today adorns the flag of Israel.

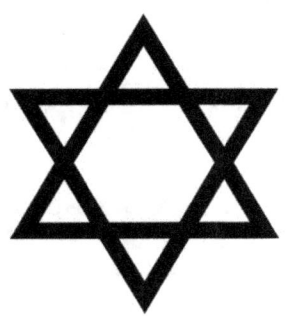

One must ask then, how is it that this graphical representation of a UFO came to be the enduring symbol of an entire nation? One that symbolizes unimaginable repression and suffering as well as an unquenchable hope.

The Ark Of The Covenant

Perhaps no ancient artifact has garnered more attention than the famous Ark of the Covenant. It has been featured in numerous novels and Hollywood films and its exact purpose, possible side effects, and indeed its current location are continuous topics of wild speculation and hot debate. What exactly is it? Well, essentially, it is a fancy box, the kapporet is its lid, and above the kapporet is the powerful merkabah (a.k.a. cherubim).

The specifications for its design are given to Moses and Bezalel, along with the tabernacle and the rest of the associated items. The Ark however plays a very central role. It could be argued that the tabernacle exists only to surround the Ark, and that perhaps the rest of the paraphernalia may also serve purposes relating to the Ark.

Traditionally, the Ark is said to be the dwelling place of Yahweh. Strangely though, the scriptures do not make that claim at all. There is a clear presentation throughout scripture of Yahweh "riding on" or "seated upon" the cherubim, as has already been discussed, and certainly, there is a connection of some sort with the cherubim and the Ark of the Covenant, but that is as much as can be said. There is no indication that Yahweh was ever inside or immediately on top of the Ark of the Covenant. In fact, several narrative sections describe the coming of Yahweh at the completion of the tabernacle. None of these narratives mention the Ark at all. Yahweh is presented as hovering over the entire tabernacle.

Exodus 40 tells of the completion of the tabernacle, and how Moses set it up, and arranged all the components. As soon as he was done, *"the cloud covered the tent of meeting, and the glory of the Lord filled the tabernacle. Moses could not enter the tent of meeting because the cloud had settled on it, and the glory of the Lord filled the tabernacle."*[137]

Later retellings of the story concur, as in the book of Numbers:

On the day that the tabernacle was erected the cloud covered the tabernacle, the tent of the testimony, and in the evening it was like the appearance of fire over the tabernacle until morning.[138]

So perhaps the Ark of the Covenant itself was not the dwelling place of Yahweh, but it did hold tremendous power. The Ark was always kept covered under a large veil especially made for the purpose. No one was allowed to touch it or even look at it. One may wonder why this would

---

[137] Exodus 40:34-35
[138] Numbers 9:15

be the case. Perhaps the secret is due to its deadly side effects.

A Dangerous Artifact

In Leviticus chapter 10, we read a very brief description of a tragic accident. The Ark of the Covenant kills Moses' nephews, Nadab and Abihu by shooting fireballs at them. The reason for this disaster is that they used "strange fire", somehow deviating from the prescribed detailed methodology. The story is relayed in a very perfunctory manner, with surprisingly little to indicate any sense of wrongdoing or punishment. It all seems very matter of fact, as though a simple mistake led to an unforeseen, yet completely understandable consequence.

Shortly before this incident, these two men had been among the 70 elders of Israel who had had the honor of feasting with the Elohim in their spaceship as described in Exodus 24. They had literally been in the presence of god with no ill effects, yet now they are blasted by the ark because they messed up the safety protocols. The ark does not appear to respond with rage or jealousy, but merely as a physical consequence. Rather than an angry god, this appears to be a situation more akin to many safety protocols we would recognize today, such as "no smoking while pumping gasoline". It is less of a "rule" and more of a case of simple common sense. Gasoline is highly flammable and relatively volatile, so an open flame in the vicinity of gasoline vapors is a risky situation that should be avoided. It may have been a similar situation with Nahab and Abihu.

Neither is this an isolated incident. A number of similar events are recorded in the Biblical account. In 2 Samuel chapter 6, a priest named Uzzah inadvertently touched the ark, in a reflexive attempt to stabilize it after the cart it was on hit a bump in the road. He was immediately struck dead.[139] On another occasion, a crowd of onlookers watched as an unsanctioned ceremony was performed with the ark, and again, the safety protocols were not strictly followed, resulting in at least seventy[140] deaths.[141] After these events, King David ordered the Ark to be kept far away, in an isolated village in the countryside.[142] Clearly, David regarded the ark itself as a dangerous artifact, rather than taking the view that the people themselves had upset god.

A Weapon

The power and danger of the Ark is further demonstrated by the fact that the armies of Israel employed it as a weapon against their enemies.

During the Battle of Jericho, the Ark played an instrumental role in destroying the walls of the city, although admittedly it is not possible today to fully understand precisely how this was accomplished. According to Joshua 6, the Ark was carried around the city once a day for six days, accompanied by the army and seven priests blowing trumpets made of ram horns. On the seventh day, the seven priests sounding the seven trumpets before the Ark compassed the city seven times and, with a great shout, Jericho's wall crumbled, allowing the Israelite army to ransack the city.

Many years later, as told in 1 Samuel chapter 4, the army again brought the ark into battle, confident that it would ensure their victory. Alas, this time the battle did not go well, and the Ark was captured by the Philistines. When

---

[139] 2 Samuel 6:3-7

[140] Some manuscripts give the number of deaths in this particular instance as 50,070

[141] 1 Samuel 6:1-19

[142] 2 Samuel 6:9-10

the Philistines tried to use this powerful weapon, it somehow backfired on them, releasing a plague of painful skin diseases upon them.[143]

The Hornet

The Ark of the Covenant was not the only weapon provided by Yahweh during the Exodus. Yahweh sends Moses a weapon called "the Hornet".

I am sending one with you to guard you along the way and to bring you to the place I have prepared. [...] Do not rebel against him; he will not forgive your rebellion, since my power is in him. [...] I will be an enemy to your enemies and will oppose those who oppose you. [...] I will wipe them out. [...] I will send my terror ahead of you and throw into confusion every nation you encounter. I will make all your enemies turn their backs and run. I will send the hornet ahead of you to drive the Hivites, Canaanites and Hittites out of your way.[144]

The word translated as 'hornet' הַצִּרְעָה (hassirah) appears to be closely related to the word for leprosy,[145] צָרַעַת (saraat), which is interesting, given the experiences of the Philistines and their outbreaks of painful skin lesions.

Yahweh later repeats his promise to send this weapon along with Moses, in Exodus 33:14, where we read *"My Presence will go with you, and I will give you rest."* Yet again mistranslation has crept in, for the Hebrew actually says no such thing. Rather than 'my presence', we find a Hebrew word we are already well acquainted with. פָּנַי (panay) in verse 14, and then פָּנֶיךָ (panakah) in verse 15, are versions of the word 'panim'. Of course, by now you

---

[143] 1 Samuel 5:6-12

[144] Exodus 23:20-28

[145] often used for any generic, generalized, or otherwise undiagnosed skin lesions, boils, pox, etc.

will probably recognize that this is the same word used by Ezekiel, when describing the multifaceted Merkabah. The same word which we have discovered to mean "face", or "edge/surface". Thus, according to Exodus 33:14, the "Hornet" is none other than the Cherubim described by Ezekiel, and described by Isaiah as the Seraphim, which we now realize is also the Merkabah. The Cherubim/Merkabah/Seraphim/Hornet is now revealed to possess weapon-like qualities. But not only 'qualities' but actual weaponized *intent*. The merkabah is *sent as a weapon*.

Furthermore, Yahweh explicitly promises Moses that he will *not be going with them personally* but will instead send one of his 'messengers' (malakim - the same word already explored in "Two Camps"). Here, in Exodus 33, Yahweh continues: *I will send [the messenger] before you and drive out the Canaanites, Amorites, Hittites, Perizzites, Hivites. Go up to the land flowing with milk and honey. But **I will not go with you**, because you are a stiff-necked people and I might destroy you on the way." [...] **If I were to go with you even for a moment, I might destroy you.**[146]*

Yahweh's promise is confirmed after the fact. He did in fact send a messenger, the Hornet, the Cherubim, the Merkabah. Yahweh made good on this promise, as we read several chapters later. He did indeed send the Hornet as promised. It accompanied the Israelites through all their wanderings. To be more precise, it led them. It was precisely this same object that they followed for the next forty years. The merkabah is also the "pillar of fire", and "the cloud". It is a flying object. It is not unidentified though, for it goes by many names.

In all the travels of the Israelites, whenever the cloud lifted from above the tabernacle, they would set out;

---

[146] Exodus 33:2-5

but if the cloud did not lift, they did not set out—until the day it lifted. So the cloud of the Lord was over the tabernacle by day, and fire was in the cloud by night, in the sight of all the Israelites during all their travels.[147]

It was not Yahweh himself that Moses followed through the desert for forty years. It was a floating cloud, which shone like fire at night. It was Yahweh's spaceship, his special weapon, "the Hornet".

The Slow Killer

The Hornet was indeed a deadly weapon… but perhaps not in an obvious way. The Israelites did not simply sweep in with an unbroken stream of military victories. After their entry into "the promised land" and their initial victory at Jericho, many hard-fought battles were lost, and many won. Typically, the victories were accredited to Yahweh, but it is usually not clear exactly how, if at all, Yahweh or his Hornet were implicated. We do not see descriptions of the Hornet overtaking the enemy with flames or lightning or laser beams. What we do see is a gradual overtaking of the land by the nation of Israel. This is not surprising however, because it is the way that Yahweh said it would happen, as recorded ahead of time in Exodus 23.

"I will not drive them out in a single year, because the land would become desolate and the wild animals too numerous for you. Little by little I will drive them out before you, until you have increased enough to take possession of the land. [...] Do not let them live in your land or they will cause you to sin against me, because the worship of their gods will certainly be a snare to you."[148]

---

[147] Exodus 40:36-38
[148] Exodus 23:29-33

It seems that Yahweh wanted his followers to treat the Canaanites as if they were infectious. Time and again he issued the same warning, throughout the long history of the conquest of Canaan. Yet he promised that eventually they will surely waste away. Could it be that the Hornet was waging a slow chemical war against the Canaanites, killing them slowly with radiation poisoning?

Radiation would also explain the stern warnings that Yahweh issued ad nauseum regarding staying a safe distance from Mount Sinai: *But you shall set boundaries for the people all around, saying, 'Beware that you do not go up on the mountain or touch the border of it; whoever touches the mountain shall certainly be put to death. No hand shall touch him, but he shall certainly be stoned or shot through; whether animal or person, the violator shall not live.'*[149]

In particular, the details regarding how a violator must be put to death are intriguing. Firstly, there is an unmistakable implication of inevitability. It is almost as though the person is regarded as "as good as dead already" or "dead man walking". Secondly, the executioner must keep his distance, using only projectile weapons to speed the inevitable death. Both details may indicate that the violator is infected by some fatal toxin and is highly infectious to any who may come into contact with him.

A similar situation arose on another occasion, told in the book of Numbers, as the Israelites followed the Hornet through the desert. We are told that "Yahweh sent venomous snakes among them; they bit the people and many Israelites died."[150] The critical phrase in Hebrew is הַנְּחָשִׁים (hannehasim) הַשְּׂרָפִים (ha-seraphim) וַיְנַשְּׁכוּ (way-nas-seku). This gets translated into "venomous snakes that bit". Biting here may be somewhat metaphorical. The word

---

[149] Exodus 19:12-13
[150] Numbers 21:6

'way-nas-seku' is used only a few times in the bible and does indicate literal biting in some instances, however, it is also used to describe the act of charging interest on a loan[151], which is clearly a metaphor. The word for snake, 'hannehhasim' is always translated as either snake or serpent. It is the famed "The Serpent" of the garden of Eden. Its associated imagery is heavy-laden with primeval archetypes. On top of this lies a rich symbology that would have been fresh in the minds of the Israelites, freshly immigrated as former residents of Egypt. The snake, the cobra, the pharaonic Uraeus, symbolizing authority over the land. This brings us to the third word, 'ha-seraphim'. This word occurs only in this story and in Isaiah's UFO encounter described in Isaiah 6. It was 'seraphim' that 'bit' the people in Numbers 21. As we have already seen, the seraphim is equivalent to the Cherubim-Merkabah- Hornet. The seraphim is literally the thing they are following around in the desert. Now it is clearly blamed for some kind of sickness within the Israelites themselves. There is an explicit causal connection here between the "snake-bites" (metaphorically speaking), and the UFO.

No reasons are given as to why Yahweh might be angry or intent on punishment. No sin is mentioned; not even one that can be interpreted as a simple breach of safety protocol. The standard translation would have us believe that "Yahweh sent venomous snakes among them" for no apparent reason. Why would he do such a thing? And if he did, why would he immediately give them a healing solution?[152] Did he mean to punish them or not? Clearly, this standard interpretation is somewhat problematic. Perhaps a better interpretation would be:

---

[151] three occurrences in Deuteronomy 23:19-20

[152] Numbers 21:8. This will be addressed further in a later section.

Yahweh sent the Seraphim (a.k.a. the Hornet, already established to be a dangerous weapon) with them, but it (unintentionally) harmed their own people and many died.

This certainly is in keeping with the rest of the narrative, from the harmful side effects, to being sent by Yahweh. It also clears up the obvious question of "why would Yahweh send snakes to bite the people?"

Yahweh has taken great pains to protect the people. The Hornet was sent specifically to protect them from their enemies, but it was an inherently dangerous object, so he set up strict safety protocols. He warned them time and time again about keeping their distance. He gave all kinds of safety instructions for the care and storage of this dangerous equipment. He provided them with water and food in the desert, lest they perish. In keeping with this character, the "snake bites" incident reveals not a vengeful whimsy, nor a flippant disregard for human life, but a caring and protective benefactor.

Shielding and Grounding

The elohim landed on a tall mountain, mount Sinai, and Moses climbed up and down Mount Sinai no less than seven times[153] in a fifty-day period, before a different agreement was reached with Yahweh. Rather than forcing Moses to climb the mountain all the time, Yahweh would now come down to Moses.

Before this agreement could be implemented, however, certain safety considerations had to be implemented. Moses set up a special tent called the "tent of meeting". Little detail is given regarding this tent, but we do know that it was the only place where Yahweh would

---

[153] Exodus 19:3, Exodus 19:8, Exodus 19:20, Exodus 20:21, Exodus 24:9, Exodus 24:13, Exodus 32:31

come to meet Moses. Actually, the tent was used not only by Moses, but also by Joshua.[154] It seems there was something about the tent itself that made it safe for these men to be in Yahweh's presence.

Perhaps the tent was made of some kind of protective fabric. Could it have been the same fabric that they later used in the Tabernacle, to cover the Ark of the Covenant? Was it some kind of flame-retardant or maybe a lead cloth similar to those used in today's X-Ray departments? Were the priestly garments made from the same material? Did Moses bring this fabric down from Sinai? There are many questions we simply do not know the answers to. We do however have a couple of clues.

Many items specified for the Tabernacle were to be made from hammered gold. Bezalel and the other craftsmen were to take gold, and hammer it out into a thin sheet, which would then be wrapped around the outside of certain items. The Ark was to be layered both outside and inside with this gold sheeting. These days, we use metal sheeting for a variety of purposes. Aside from purely decorative uses, two technical reasons for this practice are to provide electromagnetic shielding or grounding, or shielding from ultraviolet, X-ray, or gamma ray radiation. Electromagnetic shielding is typically achieved using inexpensive metals such as copper or aluminum, both of which are highly conductive. Radiation shielding can be made with a denser metal such as lead.

Gold combines the advantages of all these metals, in that it is very dense like lead, and very conductive, like copper. In the current market, the price of gold is approximately ten-thousand times more expensive than lead or copper. But this was not the case in Moses' day. Moses had easy access to a bountiful supply of gold, thanks to a specific series of events. Firstly, gold was highly valued

---

[154] Exodus 33:11

in Egypt and the surrounding civilizations. As such, it was mined and traded profusely, to the point that it was commonplace in the homes of the well-to-do, and to a lesser extent, even in those of the middle class. This much is evidenced by a fact revealed in Exodus.

The Israelites had already done what Moses had told them to do. They had gone to their Egyptian neighbors and asked for gold and silver and for clothes.[155]

Thus, gold was an obvious suitable and available material to use in any projects requiring radioactive shielding or electrical conductivity. The conductivity aspect becomes more apparent when considering some of the other components of the Tabernacle which called for gold thread[156], which will be further explored momentarily.

Aside from the basic materials, care is given to the act of creating airtight seals and electrically conductive joints: *And you shall overlay it with pure gold, inside and out you shall overlay it, and shall make on it a molding of gold all around.*[157]

The translation 'molding' is questionable. The word appears only in reference to this specific piece of the Ark. It is a technical term. It is not used to describe decorations on houses or temples or any other places in the Bible. The Hebrew is זֵר (zer). This 'zer' is not a decorative molding. It is a solid gold connection device; a type of socket, that tops the Ark and receives the connection from the '*kapporet*' cover, and the cherubim.

Similarly, detailed instructions are given for the clasps of the draperies for the Tabernacle. The clasps are not overlooked but are indicated as an important integral part of the overall functionality. Exodus 26 and 36 discuss in great detail the קַרְסֵי (qarsei) 'clasps' and לֻלָאֹת (lulaot)

---

[155] Exodus 12:35
[156] Exodus 39:3
[157] Exodus 25:11

'loops', and how everything must be securely fastened in multiple places with each piece connected by conductive gold clasps, to the gold plated framework, *"so that the tabernacle was a unit."*[158] This electrical isolation was somehow critical to the functioning of the tabernacle as a whole. It had to be properly connected to ensure electrical conductivity of all parts. This would allow the entire tabernacle to maintain a common voltage. The chapter goes on in similar fashion describing the boards and sockets and posts and bases made of wood, all of which are gold plated[159] to ensure electrical conductivity. All, that is, except for the bases of the frames.

The bases are what connects the entire thing to the ground. From an electrical perspective this is critically important. If the frames were connected to the ground, any electric charge within them would very quickly dissipate out, electrically neutralizing the entire construction. This is what would happen if any of the gold components were to touch the ground. This would be the desired behavior if one were attempting to block out radio interference. Since the Bible has made it clear that the structure is "one unit", it would really only take one spot to "ground out" the whole structure. So here is a fascinating fact. The bases are actually specified *not* to be made of gold. Instead, we see other materials specified. In fact, two different materials are specified for the two "layers" of enclosure around the Ark of the Covenant.

The outer tent of the tabernacle specifications call for solid bronze bases,[160] and the inner curtain surrounding the ark is to be supported on silver bases.[161] At first it may seem strange that this would be the case. The inner

---

[158] Exodus 36:13
[159] Exodus 26:29
[160] Exodus 26:37
[161] Exodus 26:32

enclosure around the ark is known as the "Most Holy Place" or the "Holy of Holies". This is the supreme "high temple" of the ancient Jewish religion. This is where you would expect everything to be the highest quality and workmanship. You would expect the most ostentatious display with no expense spared. Everything should be covered in gold! In fact, everything is. Everything, that is, except for these bases. Why? In a room full of gold-plated-everything the silver must have stood out like a sore thumb. There had to be some rational explanation as to why this was necessitated. Here we must consider the properties of these various metals. It turns out that silver is an excellent conductor, even better than either gold or copper. This can be seen in the following table:

Material	Conductivity[162]
Silver	62
Copper	59
Gold	44
Brass[163]	16
Tin	9
Bronze[164]	7
Lead	5

---

[162] measured in Siemens/m and divided by 10,000,000 to attain easily comparable factors

[163] brass is not an element, but a variable alloy

[164] bronze, like brass, is an alloy with some possible variance of composition, so it is impossible to ascertain an exact value

If electrical conductivity was the primary concern, silver is marginally the best choice. Using silver for the bases in particular would ensure an excellent ground connection and would enable the curtains to rapidly drain off any static charges that may build up. It would also shunt off any electrical fields in the area, acting as a very effective isolation shield for any kind of radio interference. It is interesting that this grounding shield is placed around the Ark of the Covenant, rather than simply grounding the ark itself by a direct connection to the ground. The ark appears to be constructed in a way that involves layers of conductive and insulating materials. Specifically, parts of it are made of wood and are coated on both sides with gold plating but assembled in such a way that might allow for two completely separated electrically isolated components. In essence, this could form areas of separated parallel conductors — a technique employed in the construction of several types of electrical components including capacitors, diodes, and even batteries. It is possible that the ark may actually have been capable of generating static electricity or interacting in some other way with any electrical fields that might have been in its proximity. The descriptions given in Exodus are quite detailed, but they do not provide enough information to prove or discredit such a theory. Recall that the text of Exodus is essentially a parts list. The actual fabrication was meant to be guided by some other documentation consisting of greater detail and diagrams *"according to the pattern **shown you** on the mountain."*[165]

If a good ground connection was so important, why then was silver not also used for the outer curtain bases? According to the chart on the previous page silver is nine times better at conducting electricity than bronze. Another way to put this is that bronze is nine times better as an electrical *resistor*. Without getting overly technical

---

[165] Exodus 25:40, 26:30

regarding the physics, suffice it to say that many types of *electronics* (as opposed to straight up electrical devices), rely less on optimizing conductivity, and more on optimizing *the differences of conductivity* between certain parts of an electrical circuit. This is why semiconductors form the basis of all electronics technologies. Is it possible then, that bronze was chosen for the bases of the outer curtain precisely because it was not as good of a conductor as gold or silver? Was it intended to "hold in" some of the electrical charge? Modern electronic circuits operate at low voltages. Five volts is the de. facto standard operating voltage for electronic circuits, including computer chips. Five volts is a very small voltage. By comparison, residential electrical circuits use 120 volts. You may have had the experience of a small jolt of electricity from a 9 volt battery. In order to get this, you would have had to stick the battery onto your tongue. 9 volts is not enough to feel with the dry skin of your fingers. Five volts is basically half that. What I am getting at is that the outer curtain may have been designed not to simply dump out all electrical charge, but to carry and retain a small voltage in the range of 5 to 10 volts. It would have been perfectly safe to touch (unnoticeable in fact) but would have been capable of driving any type of electronic semiconductor-based circuitry. Now, notice again what Yahweh told Moses about this curtain.

"Make the tabernacle with ten curtains of finely twisted linen and blue, purple and scarlet yarn, with **cherubim woven into them by a skilled worker.**[166]

It is very strange indeed that the curtain is said to contain cherubim. As we have discovered, the cherubim are equated (at least in some aspect) to the seraphim, the "living creatures", the merkabah, and the Hornet. We also ruled out the fact that they were purely decorative pictures of angels,

---

[166] Exodus 26:1-2

due to the prohibition by the ten commandments against creating "graven images".

Note that these cherubim are woven in with electrically conductive gold thread and that this work must be performed by a specially trained skilled craftsman, Bezalel, according to the designs shown him on the mountain when he was aboard the ship for a forty day training course. Add to this fact the prescription for certain types of colored threads. Could these threads also be some kind of semiconductor material? What we have here is a very specifically woven pattern, made of threads of varying conductivity. It is a grid-like pattern of connectivity involving layers of interconnected subpatterns. This is exactly the same way that electronic circuits are made. We use copper traces in layered grid-like substrates to connect subcomponents made in essentially the same way on a smaller scale with etched silicon circuits. Even if they weren't designed to be, these curtains literally would have acted as electronic circuits of unknown function, simply by the nature of the materials used and the general structure employed. Yahweh instructed Bezalel to create a circuit board. There is no debating this. The curtains were electrically conductive and absolutely would have created some kind of electrical effect, whether intentional or not. So the real question here is: did Yahweh create this electronic system accidentally? Or did he know what he was doing? If not an accident, what is its purpose? Is it some kind of control system for the Ark of the Covenant? And again, what is the purpose of the ark? Surely it isn't *just* a weapon, though it is dangerous.

Along with this systemic control and shielding, Yahweh specifies protective clothing for those whose work will bring them into proximity with the dangerous items: *Tell all the skilled workers to whom I have given wisdom in such matters that they are to make garments for Aaron, for his consecration, so he may serve me as priest.*[167]

Even with all these safety precautions and protective gear, and control systems in place, Yahweh still cautions the people to keep a good safe distance away from the artifacts, specifying that they must keep a distance of nearly a kilometer between the Ark of the Covenant and the rest of the public while travelling.[168] With all these safety protocols in mind, and having seen that Yahweh is clearly going to great lengths to protect the people and keep them safe, let us reexamine another well-known story.

The Golden Calf

Exodus 32 tells the story of the Golden Calf. The oft-told narrative can be summarized as follows: While Moses is up on the mountain, the people demand that Aaron must build them an idol to worship. Aaron acquiesces, making an idol in the form of a Golden Calf. Moses returns and freaks out, ordering the death of three thousand idolaters.

Unfortunately, several critical keys to understanding the story of the Golden Calf are generally overlooked, resulting in a greatly oversimplified narrative that is highly misleading. These factors are:
- the timing and the characters
- the materials
- the motivation
- the untrained craftsmen
- the safety requirements
- the calamity

The timing is the first piece of evidence which is often overlooked. Along with this is the question of who

---

[167] Exodus 28:3
[168] Joshua 3:4

was where, when? Moses has been up and down Mount Sinai four times already, in fairly rapid succession. On each of these trips, Yahweh has specifically given Moses very important safety information. As a matter of fact, the second and third trips were entirely devoted to the relaying of safety protocols.

Now Moses is on his fifth trip up Sinai. On trip number five, something has changed temporarily which allows Yahweh to greatly increase the number of visitors that can safely be accommodated. He invites Moses, plus his close advisors, plus seventy elders of Israel, a total of over seventy-five people.

A few details are missing from the narrative, but we know that Moses stays on the mountain for forty[169] days. We also know that the rest of his mountaineering party does not stay on the mountain the whole time. We know this because Aaron is down in the camp, heavily involved in the whole golden calf scheme, while Moses is still on the mountain. This is alluded to by Moses himself upon parting, as he tells his team "Aaron and Hur are with you, and anyone involved in a dispute can go to them."[170]

Just as the narrative does not indicate exactly how Aaron got back down to camp, it also does not indicate exactly who went back down with him and who remained on the mountain with Moses. There is some indication that Joshua stayed on the mountain the entire time. This is evidenced by several facts: Exodus 24:13 states that Joshua was with Moses when he went up, even though Joshua was not listed in verse 9 among the larger party who went up. We know Josua was there, so why is he missing from verse

---

[169] To be precise, it may have been either 40 or 46 days, depending on how one interprets the details of verse 16 and 18 of Exodus chapter 24. It is not clear whether the time periods mentioned are consecutive or overlapping.

[170] Exodus 24:13-14

9? Verse 9 mentions only Moses Aaron, Nadab, Abihu, and the seventy elders. Additionally, Joshua is conspicuously absent from camp during the golden calf incident. Another character who seems to be missing from camp is Bezalel, the master craftsman. Why in the world would Aaron take it upon himself to sculpt a statue if Bezalel, the official master craftsman, had been available? It is highly likely that Joshua was with Moses on the mountain for the whole forty days. This seems to be what the narrative indicates. *Then Moses set out with Joshua his aide, and Moses went up on the mountain of God.*[171] *Then Moses entered the cloud as he went on up the mountain. And he stayed on the mountain forty days and forty nights.*[172]

    The narrative is focused on Moses, which makes sense, since Moses is the hero of the story. Here and there, other minor characters are either mentioned or left out. Joshua is "his aide", so it seems reasonable that the narrator can simply assume that we realize he is with him. However, it leaves room for further questions. Were there other minor characters along with Moses that were not mentioned in either verse? I strongly suspect that Bezalel was indeed with Moses up on the mountain, receiving his own course of training in the technological specifics required to build cherubim.

    During this forty-day period, at the very least, we know that Moses and Joshua are on Mount Sinai. They are not simply sitting on a bleak rocky mountain top surrounded by smoke and fire, starving to death. They are inside a beautiful and well stocked spaceship, with a good kitchen and a dining hall, one that can accommodate a feast for at least seventy-five people. Are they just hanging out? That seems doubtful. Rather, there is activity going on. For one thing, we know that Yahweh is preparing a "stone

---

[171] Exodus 24:13
[172] Exodus 24:18

tablet"[173] for Moses to take back to camp.[174] Why it would take forty days for Yahweh to make a tablet is anyone's guess. It is also during this period that Yahweh is preparing the instructions, blueprints, and materials lists for the Tabernacle and its contents and related paraphernalia.

I strongly suspect that some of this documentation was being relayed back down to camp during the forty days. What evidence is there for such a claim? In Exodus 32, Aaron is in camp while Moses is still up on the mountain. Some citizens start a rumor that Moses won't be back and persuade Aaron to take action rather than simply waiting indefinitely. What does Aaron do? He immediately starts gathering gold from the people. Interestingly, this would be step one in the official Tabernacle project. The materials lists called for large quantities of gold. It would be needed for the Ark, the Cherubim, the boards and posts of the Tabernacle, and several of the other components. How did Aaron come to this decision? Was it possible that he already had a vague idea of what the plans would entail? Care must be taken with this assumption. We know that there is not some kind of daily status report flowing down the mountain. We know this because:

[the people] gathered around Aaron and said, "[...] As for this fellow Moses who brought us up out of Egypt, we don't know what has happened to him."[175]

We also know that Aaron had initially gone up Sinai and had feasted with Yahweh. It is entirely possible that at this initial meeting, some initial information had been revealed regarding the plans going forward. For example, the seventy elders would have been informed that Moses and Joshua (and possibly a few others) would be staying on

---

[173] this item will be discussed in greater detail in a subsequent chapter

[174] Exodus 24:12

[175] Exodus 32:1

the mountain for an extended period. It is highly likely that some concept of a building plan was revealed, and that likely included the fact that gold would be used in its creation. Thus, it would make sense that Aaron already knew to gather gold from the people, and also knew that some type of object needed to be made.

I therefore conjecture that when the people and Aaron brought up the idea of making this so-called golden calf, they may have actually been acting in good faith, simply chomping at the bit while attempting to follow Yahweh's plan to the best of their ability. Careful examination of the words used by the people and by Aaron reveal that once again some translation issues may be skewing the traditional narrative.

Typically we read "Come, make us gods who will go before us." Several key words play a factor in understanding the exact nature of this request; עֲשֵׂה (aseh), יֵלְכוּ (yeleku), לְפָנֵינוּ (lepanenu). and of course Elohim, the plural god-race.

Focussing first on the phrase "make us gods", we find some problematic translation. The implication inherent in this translation is clearly that of the fashioning of an idol. It is presumed that the people intend to worship this idol that Aaron makes for them out of gold. To be sure, this aspect of the story appears to be consistent, at least in part, for Yahweh himself later observes that the people are honoring the object inappropriately. Yet, one may get the feeling that there is another aspect of this act that is lost in translation. There appears to be some subtle differences and lost nuances. The word 'aseh' does not actually mean 'make'. It is not the word used when speaking about the plans to make the tabernacle and its components. It is not used when speaking of making the cherubim or the Ark of the Covenant. Rather it is a generic action word. It literally means 'do'.

Even more importantly, many of the standard translations insert the word 'idol' into this verse. This is pure fabrication on the part of the translators. The verse in no way contains or indicates any word that can be interpreted as 'idol'. The object of the sentence is 'elohim'.

What the people ask of Aaron is absolutely not "make us an idol", but rather, "do elohim for us", or "enact elohim for us." They have seen and heard the elohim descend upon the mountain in smoke and fire. They have heard the voice of the elohim. Now, as days and weeks and months are passing, they appear to have been left out of the loop. Moses is missing in action. No one is telling them what's happening. They begin to doubt whether Moses will ever return. Although they could not handle it when the elohim spoke to them directly, and begged Moses to intercede, now they miss the elohim. They long again for that connection. So they beg Aaron to do something. They beg him to fill in the gap somehow. They convince him to get started on this big project they have all heard rumours about. "What are we waiting for?" they cry, "If Moses isn't coming back, then *you do elohim for us!*"

The Israelites do not expect some little golden figurine of a cow to supplant the great and awesome power of the fiery mountain looming up beside them! On the contrary, they are trying to the best of their knowledge to begin building the mysterious devices that they have been promised. This is further evidenced by the next phrase. The phrase "yeleku lepanenu" is translated something to the effect of "it shall travel before us". This was Yahweh's plan and his message. He has promised as much. He told them he was going to send his Hornet, his Cherubim, his Merkabah. He promised it would lead them. Yet here they are sitting stationary by the same mountain, more than a month later, with very little information forthcoming and not much leading taking place.

The people desperately desire something to incite action and direction — something to travel before them. They are facing the prospect of a barren desert, far from home. They are demoralized. Their leader seems to have abandoned them. They want desperately to get on with it, though their concept of what "it" is is admittedly vague. At this point they are willing to try anything they can. So they forge ahead.

So Aaron, did... something. Exactly what is not particularly clear. It is not simply cut and dry to say that he formed a sculpture. The text is not as clear as we assume. Several of the words used may imply that Aaron was actually writing cuneiform on a clay tablet rather than forming a three-dimensional cow statue, but there is clearly some kind of connection with whatever Aaron made, and a calf. Calves are sometimes used figuratively in scripture to symbolize spring and new birth. This might play into this description of Aaron's work. Another interesting connection is that when Ezekiel encountered his first UFO, he described the cherubim as having feet "like calves".

Another word that stands out is מַסֵּכָה (mas-se-kah). It might mean 'molded' or 'molten'. This implication is somewhat at odds with the previous verse which tends to imply engraving or carving. However, 'mas-se-kah' is a strange word with a lot of other possible meanings, including 'an image', or 'a libation'[176], 'a blanket'[177], 'a veil'[178], or 'an alliance'[179].

The point here is that this passage is definitely not straight forward in its meaning. We are kidding ourselves if we think we can clearly translate it in an obvious way. This complexity continues in the next snippet. Aaron next

---

[176] https://biblehub.com/hebrew/4541.htm
[177] Isaiah 28:20
[178] Isaiah 25:7
[179] Isaiah 30:1

tells the people, *"These are your gods, Israel, who brought you up out of Egypt."* Why would he assign credit for past actions to something he just finished making? Is anyone going to believe such a ludicrous claim? He then calls for a feast and a big party, but as he does so, he specifically calls it a feast to Yahweh.[180] If the feast is explicitly specifically dedicated to Yahweh, how can we interpret this as idolatry?

Somewhere in this confusion Aaron did something wrong. I don't know what it was. I don't know if the whole idea of starting the project without official signoff was a major issue. I don't know what kind of quality one could expect given Aaron's lack of proper technical training and the lack of the finished blueprints. I don't know if perhaps Aaron just had no idea what he was getting into and did something very dangerous, given the lack of instructions to follow which seem to include a lot of very specific safety protocols.

Is it possible that Aaron's blunder was in that he endangered or possibly even infected the onlookers somehow? Was Yahweh angry because his people's lives were being toyed with? Why exactly did Moses kill three thousand men?[181] After Moses killed three thousand, the rest of the crowd became stricken with some kind of plague.[182] Was Moses simply mercy-killing the worst-affected? Was this some kind of radiation poisoning? Admittedly, this passage is troubling, and perhaps there are no clear answers.

Other Technology

Much has been said about the dangers and possible military uses of the Ark of the Covenant, the Hornet, and

---

[180] Exodus 32:5
[181] Exodus 32:28
[182] Exodus 32:35

other various aspects of the objects described in the Bible. The following section will discuss other applications involving strange, seemingly otherworldly powers. We shall examine first a few aspects of the Ark of the Covenant, then some other, lesser-well-known artifacts.

In the first book of Samuel the prophet, the Ark of the Covenant appears to have the ability to travel by itself, or at least, to navigate itself, and somehow communicate these navigational directions mentally to animals.[183] It is placed onto a cart pulled by a pair of oxen, and miraculously travels by itself straight back to Bethshemish. The Ark's navigational prowess is explicitly incorporated into the national plan by Joshua - *"When you see the ark of the covenant of the Lord your God, and the Levitical priests carrying it, you are to move out from your positions and follow it.* **Then you will know which way to go, since you have never been this way before.**[184] The Ark also seems to exhibit telekinetic abilities, when it repeatedly topples a statue in the temple of Dagon.[185]

The combination of these skills is reminiscent of Ezekiel's description of the actions of the cherubim. As we have already seen, he explicitly states that the cherubim and the wheels moved together, and the ship seemed to be controlled by the will of the cherubim. On several occasions the Ark was "consulted" for advice in decision-making or perhaps more accurately, fortune-telling.[186] Did the Ark or the cherubim that covered it hold some type of artificial intelligence?

When the Israelites finally reached the banks of the River Jordan, just across from the "Promised Land", the Ark caused the river to dry up, allowing the crowd to ford

---

[183] 1 Samuel 6:7-16
[184] Joshua 3:3
[185] 1 Samuel 5:1-5
[186] Judges 20:26-28, 1 Chronicles 13:3

the riverbed.[187] Oddly, Moses and his followers had experienced this type of thing before. Upon fleeing Egypt, the Israelites had crossed the Red Sea, also on dry land, as the waters had miraculously parted for them. On that occasion, they did not have the Ark of the Covenant. The Ark had not yet been built. On that occasion it was said that Moses' staff was responsible. However, this too may be an oversimplification of the story. There's actually a lot going on involving numerous components, including, the Hornet/Cherubim, flying lights, and mighty wind, as well as Moses' staff and his own volition.

*Then the Lord said to Moses, "**Why are you crying out to me?** [...] **Raise your staff** and stretch out your hand over the sea **to divide the water** [...] Then the **angel of God, who had been traveling in front of Israel's** army, [...] went behind them. The **pillar of cloud** also moved from in front and stood behind them, coming between the armies of Egypt and Israel. Throughout the night **the cloud brought darkness to the one side and light to the other side**; so neither went near the other all night long. Then **Moses stretched out his hand** over the sea, and all that night **the Lord drove the sea back** with a **strong east wind** and turned it into dry land. The waters were divided, and the Israelites went through the sea on dry ground, with a wall of water on their right and on their left. [...] the **Lord looked down from the pillar of fire** and cloud at the Egyptian army and threw it into confusion. [...] Then the Lord said to Moses, "Stretch out your hand over the sea so that the waters may flow back over the Egyptians and their chariots and horsemen." Moses stretched out his hand over the sea, and at daybreak the sea went back to its place.*[188]

Several points bear mentioning here. Firstly, we have already examined the pillar of fire, and have come to

---

[187] Joshua 3

[188] Exodus 14:15-27 (abridged)

find that Yahweh calls it the Hornet, and that he promised to send it to lead the Israelites when they departed from Mount Sinai. We have also seen that this Hornet, was the same object that was later experienced by both Ezekiel and Isaiah, and that they equated it with the cherubim.

What has not been mentioned thus far is that this same object was already present *before* the thunderous appearance of the mothership on Mount Sinai. In fact, as soon as the Israelites left Egypt, this fiery pillar was already leading them. The following snippet is from Exodus chapter 13, immediately after their escape from Egypt, before they even crossed the Red Sea.

By day the Lord went ahead of them in a pillar of cloud to guide them on their way and by night in a pillar of fire to give them light, so that they could travel by day or night. Neither the pillar of cloud by day nor the pillar of fire by night left its place in front of the people.[189]

One wonders then, was this object also the object that spoke to Moses from the "burning bush"? Is this what Moses has been following the whole time? And how do we rectify the fact that *this is the cherubim* with the fact that the cherubim are to be made by Bezalel and placed upon the Ark? It is also becoming more clear than ever that the text of Exodus does not always differentiate when a given object or phenomena *is* or *is not* actually equated with Yahweh. Chapter 13 appears to equate the pillar of fire with Yahweh, but in chapter 33 Yahweh explicitly states that he is not coming with them, but sending the Hornet, a.k.a. the pillar of fire instead.

The question of "who is doing what" is not always one that we might have answers to. There appears to be discrepancies baked right into the original Hebrew text. These are not merely translation issues but appear to be derived from a lack of clarity on the part of the original

---

[189] Exodus 13:21-22

authors. Not surprising, considering the strange phenomena that Moses had witnessed. Perhaps a few details can be followed though. The parting of the Red Sea and of the Jordan River are quite similar, but they also contain telling differences. At the Red Sea, the pillar of fire is not the cause. The pillar of fire moves away from the sea, to position itself as a rear guard between the Israelites and the Egyptian army. It is Moses who approaches the sea, with his staff. At this point Yahweh essentially denies responsibility as well. He says to Moses, "Why cry to me? Raise your staff!". Moses and his staff are clearly the cause of the Red Sea parting. Not Yahweh, nor the cherubim.

When they come to the Jordan River, again neither Yahweh nor the cherubim appear to be the cause. This time we are told that the Ark of the Covenant is the cause. However, we must realize that by now, the Ark has been activated, and it too is said to have a cherubim component. Has the power or perhaps the programming of Moses' staff somehow been transferred into the Ark? Or perhaps into the cherubim atop the Ark?

The opening chapters of the book of Joshua are all about transferal. Chapter 1 tells of the leadership and authority of Israel passing to Joshua after the death of Moses.[190] It speaks of the transferal of territory[191] and of a generational transferal from the previous generation, from Moses and Aaron and the original elders of Israel, to the next generation.[192] At this point, we are also told that miraculous manna stopped, for the new land would provide food for them. (Joshua also briefly mentions an encounter with an otherworldly humanoid[193], but sadly, there is not a lot to work with in his retelling.) Chapter 3 seems to show

---

[190] Joshua 1:1-2
[191] Joshua 1:3-4
[192] Joshua 5:2-7
[193] Joshua 5:13-15

a transferal of power into the Ark. What previously only Moses could do, the Ark now does. Instead of following the pillar of fire, the Israelites are now told to follow the Ark. The safety protocols, formerly employed for the pillar of fire, are now shifted onto the Ark. — *"When you see the ark of the covenant of the Lord your God, and the Levitical priests carrying it, you are to move out from your positions and follow it. [...] But keep a distance of [1 kilometer] between you and the ark; do not go near it."*[194]

After this point, we no longer hear of the pillar of fire. It mysteriously vanishes from the narrative without so much as a goodbye. This is doubly odd considering that Yahweh had promised it would go before them into the promised land to subdue their enemies. Perhaps that is exactly what it did. Perhaps it left, in order to go throughout the land ahead of the Israelites, but far ahead and without waiting for them to follow any longer. It seemed to have a new mission. In some way, it went on with it, acting out its predefined task. If anything, this highlights the odd behavior that the Hornet had exhibited up until this point. Before reaching the promised land, what exactly was the mission of the pillar of fire? Why did it seem to drift around in the desert for so long? Why did it remain stationary at times? Was it performing scans and detailed scientific analysis? If so, what might it have been looking for?

Another clear case of transferal occurs much later, between the prophets Elijah and Elisha. The circumstances are eerily similar, as well, with both prophets miraculously parting the Jordan river using Elijah's cloak.[195] Had this cloak somehow taken on the power formerly possessed by the Ark?

---

[194] Joshua 3:3-4
[195] 2 Kings 2:7-14

The Stone Tablets

Thus far, we have examined numerous flying objects that seem to have come to earth from elsewhere, and other artifacts that had been fashioned after otherworldly designs presented to Moses and Bezalel upon mount Sinai. We now turn our attention to a rather different artifact: the "stone tablets" that God gave to Moses, and Moses carried down the mountain. These tablets are commonly believed to have been literally made by Yahweh himself, and they are supposed to have been a hardcopy of the ten commandments. The Bible does seem to indicate that, however, there may be more to the story, which bears further investigation.

In chapters 20 to 23 of the book of Exodus, Yahweh gives Moses a lot of information, including, but not limited to, the famed "Ten Commandments". After hearing all this information, Moses writes it all down, according to Exodus 24:3-4; *When Moses went and told the people all the Lord's words and laws, they responded with one voice, "Everything the Lord has said we will do."* **Moses then wrote down everything the Lord had said.**[196]

The next morning, Moses reads back again what he had just written: *Then he took the Book of the Covenant and read it to the people. They responded, "We will do everything the Lord has said; we will obey."*[197]

It seems that Moses came up with a pretty good title overnight, as he now calls his writings "The Book Of The Covenant". This seems appropriate, since the people all publicly agreed to it as a binding promise. They did so in the evening after hearing it being transcribed to Moses, then they did so again after Moses read back his transcribed copy.

---

[196] Exodus 24:3-4
[197] Exodus 24:7

Here is where the story takes a strange twist. Just a few short verses later, Yahweh says to Moses *"Come up to me on the mountain and stay here, and I will give you the tablets of stone with the law and commandments I have written for their instruction."*[198] What is Yahweh talking about? Moses already had the "Book of The Covenant". He had written it the previous evening. Then he read it publicly that morning. So why does Yahweh promise to deliver another book? And why does he have to write it by hand, when he had literally just finished transcribing it to Moses. Something doesn't add up. The Book of the Covenant was transcribed by Yahweh and written by Moses. The process took maybe a couple of hours at most. Our present version (Exodus chapters 20-23) takes up less than ten pages. It's just not that long. As far as books go, it's more of a pamphlet than a book. Yet somehow, the next "book" that Yahweh writes for Moses takes forty days to make? Yes, this process occurs during the forty-day stay on the mountain, at the same time that Bezalel is likely being trained. Could this new book be some form of technical documentation, rather than the brief legal summary that Moses already wrote? Of course this makes sense. We already know that Yahweh is preparing the technical documents for the building of the Tabernacle, the Ark of the Covenant, the cherubim, etc. He even tells Moses specifically to keep the documentation with the Ark. *Place the cover on top of the ark and put in the ark the tablets of the covenant law that I will give you.*[199]

Despite what you may have seen in a certain Hollywood portrayal, the "stone tablets" and the "Ten Commandments" are absolutely not one and the same. They were created at separate times by separate authors using different technologies and for different purposes.

---

[198] Exodus 24:12
[199] Exodus 25:21

These are two very distinct and completely separate documents, if the stone tablets are even documents at all. Yet, there does seem to be some kind of relation between them, judging entirely by their nomenclature. Yahweh calls the stone tablets "tablets of the covenant" and Moses' book is called the "Book of the Covenant". Clearly, they are related. This does not mean that the content is the same, however.

If you have ever purchased a laptop or phone or even a newer vehicle, you may have gotten a "Quick Start Guide" with it. It was most likely between one and ten pages long. Much of the information was likely superfluous, but there may have been a few handy tips that proved useful upon using your device for the first time. On the other end of the spectrum exists a category of document known as the "Technical Manual" or the "Administrators Guide". It is not uncommon for such a manual to range from five hundred pages to perhaps several thousand pages. Such a manual is essentially incoherent to an everyday user, due to its highly technical and specialized focus. It is intended to be used by technicians during the course of configuration, troubleshooting, and repair. But this is merely conjecture thus far. Are there any substantial details that might shed light on exactly what the so-called "stone tablets" actually were?

The first actual physical appearance of the stone tablets, apart from Yahweh mentioning them as something he was going to do, comes at the end of Moses' forty days on the mountain. *When Yahweh had finished speaking with him on Mount Sinai, He gave Moses the two tablets of the testimony, tablets of stone, written by the finger of God.*[200] However, the phrase, "the finger of god" is actually 'the finger of the elohim'. Yahweh is not mentioned in conjunction with the tablets of stone at all. The tablets of

---

[200] Exodus 31:18

stone are explicitly stated to have been made by the elohim, rather than Yahweh himself. This fact is made all the more strange by the overall context of the chapter.

Exodus chapter 31 contains five references to Yahweh by name, plus eleven additional self-references using words 'I' or 'me', made by Yahweh within his monologue. Verse 18, in striking comparison, avoids any reference to Yahweh. Although it is Yahweh speaking and throughout the narration, he has been referring to himself by name, he here does not, but rather, credits the elohim with the actual work. This fact is reiterated in Exodus 32: *The tablets were the work of the Elohim; the writing was the writing of the Elohim, engraved on the tablets.*[201]

The fact of the matter is that the bulk of the chapter is the continuation of the subject matter that had already been taught to Moses during the forty-day training period. Verse 18 is a transitional phrase. Typically, translators may render it as beginning: "When the Lord finished speaking to Moses on Mount Sinai". This is somewhat misleading, as "the lord" implies the name of Yahweh, which is not the case at all. There is in fact no direct reference to god in the first half of verse 18. Two Hebrew verbs are used here, כְּכַלֹּתוֹ (kekalotow), and וַיִּתֵּן (wayitin) both of which are passive action verbs that do not indicate a direct actor. A few of the more accurate English translations render 'kekalotow' correctly into the phrase "and it came to pass". 'Wayitin' should be translated passively as well, into "was given", rather than "he gave". Some of the other words used here have a bit of variance in meaning as well, so that לְדַבֵּר (ledab-ber) "speaking" can also mean 'meeting', and כְּתֻבִים (ketubim) "written" is actually closer to 'recorded'. Thus, I propose a more accurate translation of verse 18: *When it came to pass that the meeting on Mount Sinai had ended,*

---

[201] Exodus 32:16

two stone tablets of the testimony recorded by the finger of the elohim, were given to Moses.

It seems fairly obvious that the two stone tablets recorded a testimony of the preceding meeting. They are a summary, or perhaps a full transcript or syllabus of the material that was presented and discussed over the course of forty days, the technical aspects of the building projects and their designs. These have just been discussed for forty days and outlined briefly in chapters 25 to 30. Even this brief executive summary version contains a lot of thick data including parts lists and technical construction specifications. The stone tablets are clearly *not* the ten commandments. They had been prepared by the elohim, not Yahweh, and given to Moses just in time for him to begin the build phase of the project. They are a final report from the planning phase.

A rather intriguing thematic connection ties chapter 31 together. It speaks of hiring, job assignments, and descriptions of duties. Then it touches upon work-life balance by implementing a work week and weekend schedule, then flows immediately into the elohim turning in their final report. Nowhere in the bible do we see a similar style of writing, that stands in stark contrast with the surrounding texts. In essence, the technical manual closes with an appendix on labour practices.

Knowing now that Moses held in his hands the exact specifications and instructions to follow in order to build the Tabernacle, Ark, Cherubim, etc., we may finally understand why Moses threw the "stone tablets" down and smashed them on the ground. He knew that the false start on the golden calf was a bad beginning for the project and he intended to stop them in their tracks. It was not a mistake they would be able to fix even with the correct instructions. Moses put a sudden "stop work order" on the builders, effective immediately, then quickly shifted gears into damage control. The instructions could not fall into the wrong hands. They had to be destroyed immediately. There was far too much at stake to allow these incompetent fools to work on such a dangerous project.[202]

The content of the stone tablets now seems clear, but what about their structure? Were they made of simple stone, or perhaps something more elaborate? Although the Biblical text gives very little extra data to work with, the Jewish Talmud teaches that they may have been made of blue sapphire — the same material as the floor of the spaceship described in Exodus 24:10, directly under Yahweh and Moses' feet when the intention to craft the tablets of the covenant is disclosed in Exodus 24:12. Jewish tradition also includes that the carving went through the full thickness of the tablets, yet was miraculously legible from both sides. This is presumably based on the biblical verse *"the tablets were written on both their sides"*[203].

Holographic Projection

The concept of a blue crystal data storage device that is visible from both sides sounds too much like a holograph to ignore. We already know that the spaceship had a blue sapphire floor, so perhaps there was other sapphire based technology as well. Referring to the Tabernacle plans, Yahweh tells Moses: *See that you make them according to the pattern **shown you** on the mountain.*[204] Again, this is repeated: *Set up the tabernacle according to the plan **shown you** on the mountain.*[205] Both verses occur in the midst of the executive summary. Both appear to refer to a visual representation or diagram or perhaps a three-dimensional model of the devices that

---

[202] see Exodus 32 and Deuteronomy 9
[203] Exodus 32:15
[204] Exodus 25:40
[205] Exodus 26:30

Moses was shown back on the ship. During the forty-day mountain-top tutorial, Yahweh used visual aids. Any good teacher knows that words are more effective when accompanied by pictures. The possible technology for such displays has already been touched upon in a previous section,[206] witnessed by the seventy-five elders of Israel.

Gazing with stunning realization upon the 'god of Israel', instead endured a machine of wood and sapphire. It was a precise depiction of the structure of the heavens, clear and wonderful.

Even the conservative online Bible seems to concur with at least the last half of my own translation: *Under his feet as it were a work of paved sapphire and it was very like the heavens in its clarity.*[207]

It was very like the heavens in its clarity. It was a precise depiction of the structure of the heavens, clear and wonderful. Such a depiction would be an absolute necessity for anyone attempting to navigate between planets. The vast distances involved would likely require some type of 'zoom' function, and the sheer geometrical complexity of three-dimensional objects such as stars and planets, and the appearance of constellations and other cosmic phenomena, all in relative motion with various orbits, spins, and the complex interactions of Newtonian physics, truly does require a dynamically updating display capable of perspective rotation and three-dimensional representation. This navigational display could very well have been a three-dimensional hologram. It may even be the original version of the cherubim.

This may be why Yahweh is said to appear upon the cherubim. Perhaps Yahweh himself is in fact a holographic representation. One cannot help but think of the iconic scene in Star Wars where Princess Leia pleads "Help me

---

[206] pages 59-62

[207] https://biblehub.com/interlinear/exodus/24.htm

Obi-Wan Kenobi. You're my only hope!" while projected holographically by R2-D2. The blue flickering image is even the same color as sapphire. Obviously Hollywood is no evidence for Biblical translation, but try to imagine the following verse looking like anything but a hologram:

There, above the cover between the two cherubim that are over the ark of the covenant law, I will meet with you and give you all my commands for the Israelites.[208] Surely this is as plausible an explanation as any as to why the supposedly omnipresent god could only appear in a very specific location within a certain proximity to a physical artifact built by a man according to plans given to him while aboard a spacecraft.

As another example, recall the shining blue-ish or greenish man encountered by Daniel, and already discussed on page 48. Holographic technology could also explain why only Daniel was able to get a clear view of the image, even though everyone else could hear it clearly. When it comes to holograms, they may be designed to accommodate only certain viewing angles. This may also account for the fact that the stone tablets were "written on two sides".

According to Exodus 25:10–22 the stone tablets were "stored" in the Ark of the Covenant, underneath the cherubim. More precisely, they were to be "inserted". One translation puts it well: *And you shall put into the Ark, the testimony that I shall give to you.*

The 'testimony' is to be placed into the Ark. The focus here is of the information contained, rather than the physical medium. The testimony must be loaded into the Ark. The Ark is not a simple box. The ark is not simply a treasure chest. It is a kinetic device of immense power. Were the stone tablets some type of data storage mechanism for the cherubim holographic projector? Were

---

[208] Exodus 25:17-22

the detailed technical manual tablets intended to be projected for Bezalel to reference during the building project?

One possible wrinkle in this theory comes in the fact that after destroying the first set of tablets, a second set was later cut by Moses and rewritten by God. *Yahweh said to Moses, "Cut two stone tablets like the first ones, and I will write on them the words that were on the first tablets, which you broke. [...] So Moses cut two stone tablets like the first ones and went up Mount Sinai early in the morning, as the Lord had commanded him; and he carried the two stone tablets in his hands.*[209]

It bears mentioning that the word 'chiseled' is used in many translations. This is entirely unsupported. The word פָּסַל־ (pesel) means "cut" and does imply any type of tool or specific technique. It may even include "flint knapping" or flaking. What we do know is that Moses was able to cut the stone between the evening on one day, and the following morning. He was clearly not doing any major chiseling or carving of a large stone tablet. The other fact we see here is that he can easily carry the stones in his hands, while climbing up a mountain. This can only mean one of two things. Either the stones were ordinary rocks but were quite small. This would give Moses enough time to cut them to whatever shape was required. However, it is not clear how a large volume of data could be fit onto a small, hand-sized stone. The other option is that perhaps they were sapphires after all. The crystalline form of gemstones is more amenable to data storage. This has been demonstrated recently by several university and high-tech research labs that have developed technologies to store data inside diamonds, quartz, and even glass, using similar techniques that exist in consumer grade CDs and Blu Ray disks. Moses and Yahweh may have been employing quartz, which is

---

[209] Exodus 34:1-4

very commonly found in ordinary rocks such as granite. On the other hand, perhaps the answer was already revealed way back in Egypt:

The Israelites did as Moses instructed and asked the Egyptians for articles of silver and gold and for clothing. The Lord had made the Egyptians favorably disposed toward the people, and they gave them what they asked for; so they plundered the Egyptians.[210]

As we shall soon discover[211], there were at least a few sapphires in amongst all that plunder.

Josua's recording stone

Another example of this technology appears in the book of Joshua, who took over leadership of Israel after the death of Moses. Joshua calls a national leadership conference and presents a final keynote address which he records on some kind of stone.

"See!" he said to all the people. "This stone will be a witness against us. It has heard all the words the Lord has said to us. It will be a witness against you if you are untrue to your God."[212]

We are not told how Joshua records the stone. Perhaps he used the Ark to record his speech onto a gemstone, then ejected the storage device, which he then stashes under "the oak tree near Shechem". The point here is that he tucks the message away safely in a very well-known publicly accessible place for future reference by anyone who deems necessary to hold the corporate decision publicly accountable. The only way that would be possible is if the "stone" literally contained the actual words of the entire agreement. Interestingly, the spot he chose was

---

[210] Exodus 12:35-36
[211] see page 134
[212] Joshua 24:27

already a well-known landmark, with an established extraterrestrial connection. It was the exact location where Yahweh first appeared to Abraham several hundred years earlier, as revered in the Hebrew oral history, and briefly mentioned in Genesis 12.

Comms

It seems quite possible that the Ark of the Covenant was capable of both projecting holographic displays and of recording audio. Might it also have included some kind of long-range telecommunication functionality? The detailed instructions for building the Ark conclude in a functional description. Yahweh tells Moses; *There, above the cover between the two cherubim that are over the ark of the covenant law, I will meet with you and give you all my commands for the Israelites.*[213]

The appearance of Yahweh above the Ark is to include a visual representation and a live audio feed by which Yahweh can give Moses updates. This is not a one-way communication either, for we see examples of the Israelites communication back to Yahweh, and even initiating the two way communication, similar to making a phone call.

And the Israelites inquired of the Lord. (In those days the ark of the covenant of God was there, with Phinehas son of Eleazar, the son of Aaron, ministering before it.) They asked, "Shall we go up again to fight against the Benjamites, our fellow Israelites, or not?" The Lord responded, "Go, for tomorrow I will give them into your hands."[214]

In this case, a man named Phinehas appeared to work as radio operator "ministering before the Ark". This

---

[213] Exodus 25:22
[214] Judges 20:27-28

is a key part of the responsibilities of the Jewish priesthood. A whole tribe of men was trained and specially equipped to clean and maintain the Ark, its associated paraphernalia, and its buildings, grounds, and operating manuals. Communication was of utmost importance to Yahweh. He spends a good deal of effort to ensure the availability of continued communications. Even before the Ark was built, Yahweh seems to have provided some form of temporary two-way radio set.

Moses used to take a tent and pitch it outside the camp some distance away, calling it the "tent of meeting." Anyone inquiring of the Lord would go to the tent of meeting outside the camp. And whenever Moses went out to the tent, all the people rose and stood at the entrances to their tents, watching Moses until he entered the tent. As Moses went into the tent, the pillar of cloud would come down and stay at the entrance, while the Lord spoke with Moses. Whenever the people saw the pillar of cloud standing at the entrance to the tent, they all stood and worshiped, each at the entrance to their tent. The Lord would speak to Moses face to face, as one speaks to a friend. Then Moses would return to the camp, but his young aide Joshua son of Nun did not leave the tent.[215]

This short passage reveals much about the early communication protocols used before the Ark was completed. Moses would go to the tent of meeting, which was manned "twenty-four-seven" by Joshua. His doing so caused a public commotion as everyone came to watch what they knew would happen next. Moses would make an initial radio call from the tent, and shortly thereafter, Yahweh's "pillar of cloud" would come down from the mountain to facilitate further communication with Moses. This pillar of cloud may or may not have been the same UFO that would later lead the people through the desert,

---

[215] Exodus 33:7-11

and become known as "the hornet", but it was definitely some type of similar flying craft that was a lot smaller than the main vessel perched atop Sinai. It enabled Moses and Yahweh to speak "face to face". In other words, it was a flying mobile video-conferencing device.

Even without the pillar of cloud present, Moses and Joshua possessed some kind of smaller, audio-only device that remained within the tent at all times. It was this device that required Joshua to remain at the tent. It was this device that was used to call the pillar of cloud down. Joshua also used the device to allow anyone from the community to "place a call" to the Elohim to ask questions, or as Moses puts it, to inquire of the lord. The tent of meeting was superseded by the Ark, and Joshua's temporary job as radio operator then passed to the priests.

The Urim and Thummim

The special equipment and training of the priests for their new role occupies a significant portion of the lengthy detailed instructions section of the book of Exodus. Specifically, in chapter 28, we find details about the "priestly garments" which appears to include communications devices, as well as safety equipment. Ostensibly, they are presented as simply clothing: *These are the garments they are to make: a breastpiece, an ephod, a robe, a woven tunic, a turban and a sash.*[216]

The section begins by referencing "the skilled workers to whom I have given wisdom".[217] This phrase refers to Bezalel and his team of craftsmen, which is a little odd, given that Bezalel is highly trained in metallurgy and other more high-tech crafts. Why would he be required on a simple textiles project? All the Israelites would have been

---

[216] Exodus 28:4
[217] Exodus 28:3

accustomed to making their own clothing and tent fabrics. It seems like a terrible waste of resources to assign such a task to Bezalel, when literally anyone could have pulled this off. Even if it were simply a matter of demanding the highest quality work for the holy garments, surely there were other skilled weavers and tailors equal to the task at hand. The clue comes in the following verse: *Have them use gold, and blue, purple and scarlet yarn, and fine linen.*[218] It's the gold yard. Gold; that highly conductive metal from which cherubim are woven. Perhaps these are not just simple garments after all. The next couple verses take care to ensure electrical conductivity between various pieces: *Make the ephod of **gold**, and of blue, purple and scarlet yarn, and of **finely twisted** linen—the work of **skilled hands**. It is to have two shoulder pieces attached to two of its corners, **so it can be fastened.** Its **skillfully woven** waistband is to be like it—**of one piece** with the ephod and **made with gold**, and with blue, purple and scarlet yarn, and with finely twisted linen.*[219] This focus continues in verses 9 to 14 with numerous mentions of gold filigree settings, fasteners, attachments, and braided chains of pure gold. Whatever technology was woven into the tent fabric circuitry was used again here in the priestly wearable tech.

The next piece detailed is perhaps one of the most fascinating and mysterious objects in the Bible. It is to be made with twelve gemstones. Some of their exact identities may be debated, but they are commonly thought to include emerald, topaz, turquoise, agate, amethyst, jasper, diamond, and sapphire.[220]

Thus, we now know for a fact that sapphire was among the list of required and available building materials for the Tabernacle project, and very likely could have been

---

[218] Exodus 28:5
[219] Exodus 28:6-8
[220] Exodus 28:15-19

the stones used by Yahweh and Moses for encoding the technical manuals, as speculated in previous sections.[221]

Each of these twelve stones are to be engraved, with a coded word corresponding to the twelve tribes of Israel[222], the primary division for political, legal, regional, and familial purposes within Jewish culture. These appear to be color coded, due to the varying hues of the associated gemstones, and all are integrated into an electrically conductive grid. Could this be some type of computer input/output keypad? It seems to be designed to work in conjunction with the Ark of the Covenant, and/or the tabernacle curtains, for the high priest is to wear it "whenever he enters the holy place"[223] in order that he "will always bear the means of making decisions for the Israelites".[224] Furthermore, this strange item is given the name: "the Breastpiece of Decision"[225]

We now encounter a curious phrase: *Also put the Urim and the Thummim in the breastpiece*[226] The passage contains no further details or description of what the Urim and Thummim are. It seems to tell us only that they were carried in the priest's pocket. This plain fact is reiterated several times in scripture,[227] but in each of these instances, no further detail is given. There are however several narrative passages[228] describing the actual use and functionality of the Urim and Thummim. Each of these stories show the Urim and Thummim being used as a decision-making tool, however, there is another factor at

---

[221] pages 126-130
[222] Exodus 28:21
[223] Exodus 28:29
[224] Exodus 28:30
[225] Exodus 28:15, 29
[226] Exodus 28:30
[227] Lev 8:8, Deut 33:8, Ezra 2:63, Neh 7:65
[228] Num 27:21, 1 Sam 14:41, 1 Sam 28:6

play that has been often overlooked. Let's look at each of the passages:

Num 27:21 - *And he shall stand before Eleazar the priest, who shall **ask counsel** for him after **the judgment of Urim** before the LORD*

1 Sam 14:41 - *Then Saul said, "**O Lord God of Israel!** If this sin has been committed by me or by my son Jonathan, then, O Lord God of Israel, **respond with Urim**. But if this sin has been committed by your people Israel, **respond with Thummim**." Then Jonathan and Saul were indicated by lot, while the army was exonerated.*

1 Sam 28:6 - *And when Saul **inquired** of the LORD, the LORD **answered him not,** neither by dreams, **nor by Urim**, nor by prophets.*

Each of these cases includes an element of communication for inquiry plus an answer delivered somehow via Urim and Thummim. This seems a bit more complex than the common misconception that the Urim and Thummim were two simple stones used much like dice or traditional divining bones, or the Biblical practice of casting lots. Indeed, the Urim and Thummim work in conjunction with both the twelve-gem 'keypad' and the Ark itself. All three are used together and never is one to be used outside of the Tabernacle. They are all components of a larger system.

Both words are Hebrew plural forms, as indicated by the '-im' suffix. This fact alone disproves the "two stones" theory. Had they been two stones, each referred to by a different name, each of those names would have been singular nouns, not plural.

We then note the fact that the user is not simply "asking the stones" for an answer, as one would in an oracular function, but that the question was asked verbally, to Yahweh in the presence of the Ark, and that the Urim and Thummim somehow revealed the reply from Yahweh.

An act similar to rolling dice makes no sense in the context of the complexity and holiness of the Tabernacle and all of its trappings. Instead, we see a similarity between the Urim and Thummim and the Stones of Testimony. Just as "the testimony" was loaded into the Ark, so too, the Urim (plural) and/or the Thummim (plural) were to be loaded into the breastplate with its attached gemstones. Since we are never given any indication whatsoever of any physical properties of either the Urim or the Thummim, perhaps it is naive and ill-advised to assume that they were physical objects at all. Perhaps, like the testimony, this was some kind of software or program that was to run on the gemstones or the inner workings of the so-called "Breastplate of Decision". Look how Yahweh words his instructions. *You shall put into the breastplate of judgment the Urim and the Thummim*[229] This might very well refer to the loading of data rather than an insertion of a physical object. Later, in the book of Leviticus, the action is performed: *he put into the breastplate the Urim and the Thummim.*[230]

If these were software packages, they were programmed into the ephod. The ephod is made of finely spun gold threads with explicitly described electrically conducting fasteners and with gemstones that might possibly glow under certain conditions. If these were physical objects, they were put into the ephod — why? Simply for storage? Maybe. So that they would be handy when the priest needed to use them. But they were never removed. Not once in any of the occasions when they are consulted are they ever described as being taken out, or examined, or shaken, or even spoken to. The query goes to Yahweh and the answer comes back through the Urim and Thummim while they remain inside the ephod. The Urim

---

[229] Exodus 28:30
[230] Leviticus 8:8

and Thummim only work from within the overall telecommunications system.

The Message

Close Encounters Of The 3rd Kind are essentially concerned with communications. Much attention has been given thus far in this volume to the details of the encounters themselves and to the messengers. We would be remiss not to at least touch upon the body of the message.

The message is often convoluted, specific, and mired in contextual details which have been lost to time. The message often is political, bearing hidden or not so hidden agendas. The message is sometimes harsh, judgmental, demanding, unrelenting, and violent.

Yet underneath all the bluster and fury is a subtler, gentler message. The message is encapsulated by the prophet Isaiah:

He said, "Go and tell this people:
" 'Be ever hearing, but never understanding;
    be ever seeing, but never perceiving.'
Make the heart of this people calloused;
    make their ears dull
    and close their eyes.
Otherwise they might see with their eyes,
    hear with their ears,
    understand with their hearts,
and turn and be healed."
Then I said, "For how long, Lord?"
And he answered:
"Until the cities lie ruined
    and without inhabitant,
until the houses are left deserted
    and the fields ruined and ravaged,
until the Lord has sent everyone far away

and the land is utterly forsaken.
And though a tenth remains in the land,
  it will again be laid waste.
But as the terebinth and oak
  leave stumps when they are cut down,
  so the holy seed will be the stump in the land."[231]

There is mourning for the lost opportunity, amidst the freedom to ignore. There is a warning of great cyclical calamity. Yet there is a remnant. Long after the visitation, long after most people have forgotten, long after the transferred technology has fallen out of use and fallen into disrepair, Yahweh longs for the constant communication they once shared. He descends once again to plead:

'Return to me, and I will return to you,' says the Lord Almighty.[232]

---

[231] Isaiah 6:9-13
[232] Zechariah 1:3

The 4th Kind: Abductions

A Close Encounter of the Fourth Kind is a UFO event in which a human is abducted by a UFO or its occupants. The first widely publicized UFO abduction in modern times was that of Betty and Barney Hill in 1961. Since then, many have claimed similar experiences. But the Hills were by no means the first. Written thousands of years ago, the Bible contains numerous accounts that fall into this category.

Taking Captives

As we have already seen, the psalms of David contain many references to Yahweh riding on fiery cherubim in clouds of smoke. Psalm 68 adds another layer of intrigue by implying that Yahweh actually flew his ship from Sinai to engage in battle, called in additional craft as reinforcements, and took captive prisoners of war onto his ship. An abridged version of the psalm is highlighted here:

May God arise, *may his enemies be scattered;*
 may his foes flee before him.
May you blow them away like smoke—
 as wax melts before the fire,
 may the wicked perish before God. [...]
Sing to God, sing in praise of his name,
 *extol him **who rides on the clouds**; [...]*
the earth shook, the heavens poured down rain, [...]
"Kings and armies flee in haste;
 [...] the Almighty scattered the kings in the land,
The chariots of God are tens of thousands
 and thousands of thousands;
 *the Lord comes from Sinai **in his sanctuary**.*
When you ascended on high,

> *you took many captives;[..]*
> *[...] sing praise to the Lord,*
> *to **him who rides across the highest heavens**,*
> *[...] You, **God, are awesome in your sanctuary**.*[233]

David's fascination with the cherubim is unsurprising, given that he apparently witnessed an uncountable horde of the flying machines. As described earlier,[234] Yahweh's fleet of cherubim arrived to battle and scattered the enemy. David's tone is clearly that of a man on the winning side of battle. He relishes the victory, however one-sided it may have been. His airborne allies "took many captives". This is no normal taking of prisoners. Nowhere is a landing described. We do not read of swords clashing or people being tied with ropes. We read only of Yahweh remaining "in his sanctuary", "riding across the highest heavens". Essentially, David is stating that these prisoners were somehow snatched up into the flying craft. History is written by the victors, but one has to wonder if these captives lived to tell the tale, and what that experience may have been like from their perspective.

John

The book of Revelation is perhaps one of the most studied yet least understood sections of the Bible. In this book it seems as though John is abducted into a giant mothership known as "the New Jerusalem". The narration begins like many of the other UFO encounters, with flying objects descending from the clouds. *Look, he is coming with the clouds, and every eye will see him*[235] Yet even here, we are presented with mysterious and confusing aspects.

---

[233] Psalm 68
[234] pages 66, 95
[235] Revelation 1:7

Was a crowd present to witness this event? Why does John begin this story in the future tense? In some respects, he appears to be referring to an awareness of something yet to come, but as John continues, he switches to a more prosaic narrative, which appears to be a retelling of his actual experience:

I heard behind me a loud voice like a trumpet, [...] I turned around to see the voice that was speaking to me. And when I turned I saw seven golden lampstands,[236]

The obvious implication of "golden lampstands" is some kind of glowing or fiery metallic objects. Taken with the previous statement about coming with clouds, we might assume that these objects have descended from the sky or are billowing smoke, similar to most of the Old Testament encounters.

...and among the lampstands was someone like a son of man, dressed in a robe reaching down to his feet and with a golden sash around his chest.[237]

This is an exact replica of the "Emerald Man" from the book of Daniel. John even copies the name "son of man" from Daniel.

The hair on his head was white like wool, as white as snow, and his eyes were like blazing fire. His feet were like bronze glowing in a furnace, and his voice was like the sound of rushing waters. [...] His face was like the sun shining in all its brilliance.[238]

Again, these details seem to largely concur with Daniel. It is here, however, that the similarity ends. John uses much simile to describe the scene further, some of which seems banal enough but others of which are extraordinarily difficult to follow.

---

[236] Revelation 1:12
[237] Revelation 1:13
[238] Revelation 1:14-16

The standard status quo approach to interpreting Revelation is to insert a lot of political and spiritual imagery, metaphor, and rhetoric. This approach may be at least partially appropriate, but in my opinion, it drastically misses the mark. There is just too much evidence that fits in with the physical descriptions of UFOs found throughout the Old Testament. In Revelation chapter 4 there is an abundance of description mirroring that of the ship where Moses and the seventy-five elders dined with Yahweh. John is told to "come up higher" just as Moses was. He sees a room with a floor that *"looked like a sea of glass, clear as crystal."*[239] There is a throne with a seated figure, all of which sparkled or shimmered like gemstones and rainbows[240] Twenty-four other people are seated around the room on smaller thrones[241], perhaps using the same banquet table that Moses ate at. Most surprisingly, in the room are also the very same cherubim that were witnessed by Ezekiel and Isaiah and David and that Moses followed around the desert all those years. John was clearly taken up into the exact same ship and witnessed all the same technologies as his ancestors had witnessed over a thousand years previously.

In chapter 21, it seems that this ship has somehow travelled to a different planet, and is now making a landing, for John describes: *I saw "a new heaven and a new earth," for the first heaven and the first earth had passed away, and there was no longer any sea. I saw the Holy City, the new Jerusalem, coming down out of heaven from God.*[242]

John continues with a comment from one of the extraterrestrials, containing a bit of background information on what they have in mind:

---

[239] Revelation 4:6
[240] Revelation 4:2-3
[241] Revelation 4:4
[242] Revelation 21:1-2

I heard a loud voice from the throne saying, "Look! God's dwelling place is now among the people, and he will dwell with them. They will be his people, and God himself will be with them and be their God. 'He will wipe every tear from their eyes. There will be no more death' or mourning or crying or pain, for the old order of things has passed away. He who was seated on the throne said, "I am making everything new!"[243]

Have they travelled to a new planet to plant a new colony and begin a new civilization? It is clear that there are humans aboard, for god will dwell "among the people". The new Jerusalem is a truly massive ship. It certainly had plenty of space for a large contingent of passengers. It is described as being made entirely of crystalline gemstones in an enormous cube with each side being over 2,000 km long. That's a bigger footprint than Texas or any current European country. Might these passengers have been volunteers, or might they even be the captives that David witnessed being scooped up by thousands of smaller raiding ships?

Enoch

The classic example of UFO abduction in the Bible is obviously the well-known and much referenced Enoch, Noah's great grandfather. Enoch makes one of the briefest appearances of any Biblical character. The entirety of his fame rests on two short verses within a genealogical listing. The patriarchal list tells each man's age at siring the familial heir, and at his death. In the case of Enoch however there is a notable exception. Enoch's entry contains no death record, but instead indicates that Enoch was taken away from earth.

---

[243] Revelation 21:3-5

After he became the father of Methuselah, Enoch walked with the elohim for three hundred years and had other sons and daughters. Altogether, the days of Enoch were three hundred and sixty-five years. **Enoch walked with the elohim; then he was no more, because the elohim took him.**[244]

This fact is confirmed in the New Testament book of Hebrews, which states more explicitly: *By faith Enoch was taken from this life, so that he did not experience death: "He could not be found, because God had taken him away." For before he was taken, he was commended as one who pleased God.*[245]

Enoch was never seen again. Where did he go? He was still alive and was taken physically, so he could not have simply translated into some spiritual heavenly dimension. His body had to go somewhere. Was he taken aboard a spaceship? Was he a willing volunteer? Was he perhaps the beginning of this new "New Jerusalem" colony?

Elijah

Much like Enoch, Elijah was also taken off the earth, and in his case, he was seen to travel up into the sky, the event witnessed by fifty men.[246] The typical translation reads as follows:

As they were walking along and talking together, suddenly a chariot of fire and horses of fire appeared and separated the two of them, and Elijah went up to heaven in a whirlwind. Elisha saw this and cried out, "My father! My

---

[244] Genesis 5:22-24
[245] Hebrews 11:5
[246] 2 Kings 2:7

father! The chariots and horsemen of Israel!" And Elisha saw him no more.[247]

A few of the Hebrew words used here bear further investigation. Let us back up a few verses to the introduction of the chapter in verse 1.

The verb in verse 1 is בְּהַעֲלוֹת (beha-alo-wt) and it means 'offer' or 'offering'. Yahweh offers something to Elijah. He offers to Elijah בִּסְעָרָה (basarah) 'a storm' to the הַשָּׁמָיִם (hassamayim) which might simply mean 'sky' or 'space' but, due to anthropomorphic suffix "-im" is more likely to mean "sky-people" or "space-men".

So it came to pass that Yahweh offered to take Elijah in a storm up to the space men. That sounds like a pretty cool offer. No wonder Elijah's sidekick, whose name was Elisha, swore to him essentially "there's no way I'm gonna miss seeing this"[248]

Suddenly, a fiery cherubim[249] appears! Yes, the same cherubim that Yahweh rides in the psalms — *And Elijah went up in the storm to the space-men.*[250]

As a humorous side note, the exclamation of Elisha upon witnessing this event may be the very first recorded example of a meme. As Elijah was being transported up, Elisha shouted out *"My father! My father! The chariots and horsemen of Israel!"* Many years later, Elisha himself lay on his deathbed, wasting away with an illness. The king came to visit him, perhaps to give him a final moment of joy on his dying day. The king greeted Elisha with his own words, *"My father! My father! The chariots and horsemen of Israel!"*[251] Both Elisha and the king knew that Elisha was about to die and that he was decidedly not going to ascend

---

[247] 2 Kings 2:11
[248] 2 Kings 2:4,6
[249] 2 Kings 2:11
[250] Ibid
[251] 2 Kings 13:14

into the sky as Elijah had done. Even so, this little inside joke may be the origin of the common belief that we "go to heaven" when we die. It was a meme that really went viral.

Ezekiel

Although the story of Ezekiel has already been examined it behooves us to mention him again in this section. Ezekiel makes it quite clear in two parts of his narrative that he was taken aboard a flying ship and transported a great distance from Babylon to Jerusalem and back again, a round trip of about three thousand kilometers. This craft was remarkably fast. That trip would take you over 30 hours, driving at highway speeds, yet Ezekiel finds himself there in almost no time at all.

After seeing a UFO descend, he tells us "The form of a hand took me by a lock of my hair and lifted me up"[252] Some translations imply that Ezekiel saw a hand or something that looked like a hand, but this is not the case. The Hebrew words used here תַּבְנִית (tabnit) יָד (yad). 'Yad' does mean hand, often a literal hand, but is also commonly used as a representation of power or authority. The meaning of 'tabnit' is "something similar in form or function." It does not in any way imply a visual representation. It is a functional description. Ezekiel is attempting to describe the physical feeling he felt centered on the top of his head. A giant hand did not come from heaven and grab his hair. Rather, he felt a force that seemed to pull his head, causing him to rise into the air. It lifted him "between earth and the sky". The destination was not some extra-dimensional "heaven" or "spiritual plane" or anything like that. It was between the earth (the ground) and the sky. He flew up, but not too far up. He did not rise beyond the sky. He didn't even reach orbit. He stayed well within the atmosphere.

---

[252] Ezekiel 8:3

This was accomplished by the 'ruach'; the ways, styles, and technologies of the elohim.

With this background in mind, we can now understand why Ezekiel opts for such a brief phrase to introduce his later abduction. *The hand of Yahweh came upon me and carried me with the technology of Yahweh...*[253] It actually makes sense. He already established what it looked like and felt like. He is assuming the reader is already familiar with his earlier encounter. Now he only needs to say that it happened again.

Philip

Another case of long-distance travel takes place hundreds of years later, as described in the New Testament book of the Acts Of The Apostles.

Then both Philip and the eunuch went down into the water and Philip baptized him. When they came up out of the water, the Spirit of the Lord suddenly took Philip away, and the eunuch did not see him again, but went on his way rejoicing. Philip, however, appeared at Azotus[254]

Just like Ezekiel, Philip credits the 'ruach'[255] for this transportation. In this case, it all happened so fast that no-one really got a good look or a chance to describe the event in more detail. What we do know is that Philip found himself in Azotus, a town approximately fifty kilometers away from where he had been moments ago. This distance may seem trivial to us. We can cover that ground in a half hour in a car at highway speed. But to a man on foot, it's about a ten hour walk — a long day's journey. It's not exactly the kind of thing that Philip could have

---

[253] Ezekiel 37:1

[254] Acts 8:38:40

[255] the Greek term 'pneuma' used in Acts is equivalent to the Hebrew 'ruach'

accomplished by himself, even if he had been walking in a daze. The ship that Ezekiel rode in could easily travel fifty kilometers in a matter of seconds.

Paul

The apostle Paul, author of approximately half the New Testament, seems to have had his own abduction experience. In his second letter to the church at Corinth, he makes a strange claim:

I know a man in Christ who fourteen years ago was caught up to the third heaven. Whether it was in the body or out of the body I do not know—God knows. And I know that this man—whether in the body or apart from the body I do not know, but God knows— was caught up to paradise and heard inexpressible things, things that no one is permitted to tell.[256]

Paul is intentionally vague, on top of the vagaries caused by his limited comprehension of the nature of this event. Whether it was in the body or in the spirit he does not know. He does not know if this was a physical phenomenon or some kind of esoteric trance, or even just a dream. He does however consider it important enough to mention, and to have remembered it vividly for fourteen years. My guess is that Paul knows that something real truly happened, but it was something so bizarre he can scarcely admit to believing it.

"I know a man," he says. He is being purposefully vague now. The consensus amongst bible scholars is that this man was in fact Paul himself. He claims to have been "caught up" to 'paradise', or in some translations, 'the third heaven' — the 'dwelling place of the lord'. He was spoken to by presumably otherworldly beings who told him inexpressible things — things beyond comprehension.

---

[256] 2 Corinthians 12:2-4

They even told him not to talk about it afterwards; not to tell anyone about his experience. Paul also states that these beings implanted something into his body.

> *I was given a thorn in my flesh, a messenger of Satan, to torment me. Three times I pleaded with the Lord to take it away from me.* [257]

What was this device? Clearly it caused Paul significant pain. Was it truly intended solely to torment him? That seems entirely contradictory to the grace and peace of Paul's God. Even Paul cannot bring himself to blame God for it, calling it a "messenger of Satan". Was Satan allowed to perform surgeries in paradise? I think not. No, if there were any surgical procedures involved, they must have been performed by the inhabitants of this third heaven; God and his angels.[258] Why would they do this? What was the purpose for this implanted device?

Many bible scholars equate this reference to Paul's conversion experience that is documented in the book of Acts. As Paul was travelling on foot, suddenly a light from heaven flashed around him. The light was so bright, he blindly stumbled to the ground and heard a voice speak to him.[259] His travelling companions could not see this light, but they heard the voice and were shocked and dumbfounded by the event.[260] Paul himself took three days to recover.[261]

---

[257] 2 Corinthians 12:7-8

[258] Since the New Testament is written in Greek rather than Hebrew, there is a significant loss of continuity in terms of terminology. The words Yahweh and Elohim do not appear in the New Testament but have been replaced by the generic role-based terms for "god" or "lord". Likewise, any other heavenly beings are typically referred to as "angels" rather than the Hebrew terms such as cherubim, malakim, etc.

[259] Acts 9:3-4

[260] Acts 9:7

[261] Acts 9:9

I find it difficult to rectify these two narratives. One contains bright lights and loud noises and a life-changing message to be shared. The other tells of ascensions and wonderful beings and secret messages that he is forbidden to share. What are we to make of these discrepancies? Combining the dissonant details Paul's story begins to resemble a modern day abduction testimony. Alleged abductees often tell of a bright light from the sky that captures them before they find themselves in some kind of extraterrestrial operating room. Is this what happened to Paul?

If Paul was in fact taken aboard a spacecraft and implanted with some type of device, such a device might explain Paul's penchant for receiving divine visions in the years to follow, of which there were many.[262] Was this implant some kind of newer biotechnology, or simply a more compact version of some of the same communication technology that had been given to Moses by Yahweh?

Alien DNA

The concept of extraterrestrial biological experimentation is one that is both deeply disturbing and ubiquitous in the modern UFO paradigm. Many abductees claim to have experienced some element of genetic sampling or implantation, including the harvesting of gametes (sperm or eggs) taken from their bodies. Several have even claimed to have been impregnated. With our advanced medical systems and widely disseminated knowledge of the science of genetics, this seems to be a distinctively modern idea. But is it? Or did our ancient predecessors undergo these same experiences?

---

[262] Acts 16:9-10, Acts 18:9-11, Acts 22:17–21, Acts 23:11, Acts 27:23-25

Nephilim

Genesis 6 tells of the Nephilim, a race of half-breeds resulting from the sexual union of gods and humans.

When human beings began to increase in number on the earth and daughters were born to them, the sons of the elohim saw that the daughters of humans were beautiful, and they took for themselves any women they chose. [...] The Nephilim were on the earth in those days—and also afterward—when the sons of God went to the daughters of humans and had children by them. These were the mighty men of ancient legends.[263]

These ancient legends do indeed concur, for every culture that has ancient stories inevitably speaks of hybrid demigods with great strength and often superhuman powers. This tradition is one of the most ancient and most globally spanning parts of our heritage. It is attested in the Bible and in the holy books of every ancient religion and mythology. If UFOs have in fact been visiting us from ancient times, it seems that such visits have included intimate contact with genealogical implications, whether intended for science or for pleasure. At least some of these contacts have apparently been deemed as punishable breaches of ethics, morals, or civility. The book of Jude claims that: *The angels who did not stay within their own position of authority, but left their proper dwelling, he has kept in eternal chains under gloomy darkness until the judgment of the great day*[264]

It seems that the Nephilim were the unintended result of an unauthorized breeding. Those "sons of the elohim" who were involved in this misadventure have been or will be punished by their authorities. Does this imply that perhaps there were (or are) other more legitimate scientific

---

[263] Genesis 6:1-4
[264] Jude 1:6

programs underway involving human breeding or genetic intervention? Has human evolution and the development of civilization been directed by some long-term plan designed and executed by a higher power?

Noah

Noah was a man at a critical crossroads of human history. Noah and his family were saved, salvaged from a previous world, and propelled forward to a new world to begin anew the human experience. Why him? A high-level summary of Genesis six reveals a single storyline in three steps:
1. The Nephilim are born, sullying the gene pool.
2. Yahweh is distraught, for his experiment is ruined and he has to start over.
3. He selects Noah to seed the new experiment.

According to the book of Genesis, "Noah found favor in the eyes of Yahweh."[265] How exactly did he manage this accomplishment? We are told in Genesis 6:9, and it involves a couple of factors. Firstly, Noah "walked with the elohim". The Hebrew verb is הִתְהַלֶּךְ (hit-hal-lek). It is a figurative word meaning "to hang out"[266] or "to explore"[267] It is the same word used to explain the reason that Enoch was taken. Hanging out and exploring are two activities that can be undertaken either alone, or with friends. In the case of both Noah and Enoch, we see the latter. Noah hung out with the elohim, just as Enoch had. This implies conversation and connection, getting to know one another and exploring ideas as well as the surroundings. Essentially, 'hit-hal-lek' means friendship. Friendship

---

[265] Genesis 6:8
[266] 1 Samuel 30:31, 2 Samuel 11:2, Ezekiel 19:6
[267] Genesis 13:17, 1 Chronicles 21:4

should never be discounted as part of the decision-making process. With friendship comes trust. Trust is critical in strategic planning. Yahweh is about to make a very strategic decision that will literally decide the course of mankind for the rest of human history.

The other factor at play in Yahweh's strategy is that of genetics. The typical translation grossly misses the main point, misrepresents the original text, and completely ignores this very important factor. According to one popular version:

This is the account of Noah and his family. Noah was a righteous man, blameless among the people of his time, and he walked faithfully with God.[268] This short phrase contains no less than six translation errors, which shall be examined one by one, phrase by phrase, word by word. Such a pivotal moment in the history of every human being alive today is worth the most detailed analysis possible.

"This is the account of Noah and his family" — in Hebrew is אֵלֶּה (eleh) תּוֹלְדֹת (toldot) Noah. There are only three words here, two of which are completely obvious; his name, and 'eleh' which is consistently translated 'these'. This leaves only the word 'toldot' in question. The translators have attempted to pack a lot into this one word: "the account of ... and his family". They are not completely barking up the wrong tree. 'Toldot' does carry these connotations. However, there is a subtle discrepancy. Specifically, the word seems to combine two concepts. Firstly, there is certainly a familial or genealogical aspect. This word 'toldot' appears thirty nine times in the Bible, and each time it either precedes a listing of a family tree, or it is used to refer to the records of a previously written family tree. It is all about the records of one's ancestry. This aspect is indisputable. This brings us to the second concept

---

[268] Genesis 6:9 (New International Version)

inherent in 'toldot'; it is always used in reference to the past, never the future. Just as in English we differentiate between our past *ancestors* and our future *descendants*, so it is in Hebrew. Yahweh speaks to Abraham about his descendants, but when it comes to Noah, he speaks only of Noah's ancestry. It is highly misleading to insert the phrase "and his family" into this context. Noah's wife and sons and daughters are Noah's descendants, not his ancestors. They are not mentioned here. Certainly, they play a critical role in the overall story of Noah — his story would go nowhere without them, but in terms of why Noah was chosen, they had nothing to do with the matter. The deciding factor here was in Noah's DNA. Rather than the phrase, "This is the account of Noah and his family", we should interpret the phrase as *"This is Noah's ancestry"*.

Moving on to the second phrase; "Noah was a righteous man, blameless among the people of his time" — in Hebrew is נֹחַ (Noah) אִישׁ (ish) צַדִּיק (saddiq) תָּמִים (tamim) הָיָה (hayah) בְּדֹרֹתָיו (bedorotaw). Each of these words plays a critical role in deciphering the meaning of this phrase. With so many "moving parts" it may be useful to employ a table:

Hebrew	pronunciation	meaning
נֹחַ	Noah	Noah
אִישׁ	ish	other
צַדִּיק	saddiq	righteous
תָּמִים	tamim	without defect
הָיָה	hayah	had become
בְּדֹרֹתָיו	bedorotaw	future generations

Keeping in mind that the Hebrew language uses a very different grammatical structure and word order than English, at first glance it may seem difficult to parse this into a proper sentence, but there are a few observations that can be made. Firstly, there is absolutely no basis for the translation "among the people of his time". The people of his own time are not mentioned. Rather, it is future generations or descendants that are indicated by the word 'bedorotaw'.

'Ish' is mistranslated as 'man' but it actually means 'other'. You may recall that we examined this word earlier.[269] It is the same word that indicated that Jacob wrestled with an "other". It implies a contrast against an existing comparator. It is the difference by which a thing may be defined. It is the imposing of a binary opposite. Thus, rendering the term "man" is actually the complete opposite of the intended meaning.

---

[269] page 12

'Hayah' implies a past perfect tense, referring to an event, action, or change that has already happened and become completed in the past. The phrase seems to be indicating that Noah had already become a righteous 'other' without defect for future generations. The fact that Noah would affect future generations is obviously due to his position as the "seed" by which the earth would be repopulated after the impending flood. Certainly, this position alone would be evidence enough to state that Noah "had become other", yet there may be another layer of "otherness" at play.

The ancestry of Noah was righteous, and his lineage was faultless. Did Yahweh choose Noah and his family based on genetics? Noah's genealogy was pure and good. However, this leaves us with another question. Noah had brothers and sisters — so what made *him* better than *them*? Was it because "he walked faithfully with God"

The word 'faithfully' does not belong in this sentence. It is not based on any word that appears in the Hebrew text but is simply inserted by the translator. As has already been discussed, Noah "hung out" with the elohim. There is nothing religious about it. It has nothing to do with faith. The text says nothing about Noah's actions, choices, lifestyle, ethics, or morals. It does not indicate his beliefs, rituals, or any other religious connotations. The righteousness of Noah was not action oriented. What righteous act of Noah can be pointed to before the flood narrative? None. He is not even mentioned until he is chosen to survive the flood. Not a single story exists to show his righteous actions.

We must conclude then that yes, Yahweh did use genetic data to select the best candidate with which to repopulate earth. *This is Noah's genealogy. Noah had become the righteous other without defect for future generations. He hung out with the elohim.* Two facts are presented. There may or may not be a causality implied. If

there is an implication of causality, it seems we have gotten it backward. Look at the order of the facts:
- Noah was the righteous seed.
- Noah hung out with the elohim.

We are subtly led to believe that Noah was chosen *because* he hung out with the elohim. But this is the opposite of what the text seems to say. The order is backwards. The text simply states the facts in chronological order. It does not include the word "because". What the text actually says is:

1. Noah was the righteous seed
2. Noah hung out with the elohim

Noah was important to the elohim and their plan to repopulate the earth. He was the righteous seed. His DNA had the correct attributes that made him a desirable and appropriate tool to carry on the human race. So the elohim hung out with him. They had to, to ensure his survival. They needed to give him certain information that would allow him to survive the upcoming catastrophe. They had to communicate this critical information to him somehow. You already know the rest of the story. You know it by the name of "Noah's Ark".

I realize that I am about to do something cruel at this point. I have stressed the importance of two seemingly small factors: the "otherness" of Noah, and the past perfect tense in which this otherness occurred. These points relate to additional information within the ancient records that, sadly, falls beyond the scope of this particular book. In order to flesh out this discussion and possibly draw a conclusion I would need to include additional details that can only be found within non-canonical material from the Dead Sea Scrolls. Since these apocryphal books are not considered (by much of christendom, at least) to be worthy of inclusion into scripture, and since the stated scope of this book is UFOs "In The Bible", I am unable to discuss within it this particular point any further. I will however include further material on my website for those that care to pursue the matter further.[270]

The Virgin Mary

In the first chapter of this book, we saw a group of wise men following a UFO for hundreds, or possibly thousands of miles, to a faraway land to witness a miraculous birth. The reason the birth was so noteworthy was that the mother apparently was a virgin. How can a virgin conceive? It was truly a marvel.

In light of the evidence presented thus far, and the claims of biological tampering made by the Apostle Paul as well as countless modern-day abductees, is there any reason to suppose that it might be possible that perhaps Mary, the mother of Jesus, may also have been the subject of such tampering? Could she have been taken aboard a UFO and artificially impregnated or implanted with a divine or hybrid fetus? Such claims are almost too wild to entertain, and certainly, the repercussions would be shocking. Can we, based solely on scripture, argue the case either way? Let us examine the scriptures. The virgin birth story appears in two of the gospels, Matthew and Luke. Mark does not mention it. This fact alone is somewhat odd, given that Matthew and Luke are seen by many biblical scholars to stem from the book of Mark as the original written source material.

The gospel of Matthew claims the following: *This is how the birth of Jesus the Messiah came about: His mother Mary was pledged to be married to Joseph, but before they came together, she was found to be pregnant*

---

[270] https://UFO.dimensionfold.com

through the Holy Spirit. Because Joseph, her husband, was faithful to the law but did not want to expose her to public disgrace, he had in mind to divorce her quietly. But after he had considered this, an angel of the Lord appeared to him in a dream and said, "Joseph son of David, do not be afraid to take Mary home as your wife, because what is conceived in her is from the Holy Spirit.[271]

Two significant events take place here. The second event has an angel appearing to Joseph in a dream. The first event though, is... missing. There is no mention of the miraculous event which caused Mary to be pregnant. Instead, we simply read that Mary "was found to be pregnant by the Holy Spirit[272]". This is a very strange explanation. Why do we not hear about how or why or when or where this occurred. She "was found"? What does that even mean? How can such an important event be glossed over like this? It is reminiscent of Abraham's origin story, where the actual event is missing from the story and we are simply told after the fact "something had already happened" with absolutely no detail. Thankfully, Matthew's is not the only account of the story. Surely Luke will shed more light on the subject.

Indeed, enter Luke, ever the careful and yet loquacious author. He will make all things right. He begins by stating as much explicitly in his introduction: *I myself have carefully investigated everything from the beginning. I too decided to write an orderly account for you, [...], so that you may know the certainty of the things you have been taught.*[273]

Indeed, Luke's journalistic skills are superlative, and he launches into a detailed retelling of the events leading up to Jesus's birth: How Jesus' Auntie Elizabeth

---

[271] Matthew 1:18-20
[272] the pneuma or ruach
[273] Luke 1:3-4

becomes pregnant and how Uncle Zechariah is working as a priest near the Ark of the Covenant, where he witnesses an extraterrestrial messenger named Gabriel, and how he is unable to speak for the next nine months, and what the baby will eat, and what he will do when he grows up, and how Uncle Zechariah was not very good at sign language, and how Gabriel went to visit Mary, and what he told her.

Gabriel tells Mary, *The Holy Spirit will come on you, and the power of the Most High will overshadow you. So the holy one to be born will be called the Son of God.*[274]

So far, nothing has happened *to Mary*. All she has gotten so far is visitors with messages. No pregnancies. So Luke continues; he tells about how Mary went to visit her cousin, and how they could feel her cousin's baby kicking in the womb, and about how happy they all are. Luke recites to us the lyrics of a freestyle rap that Mary performs. He tells us about the birth of Mary's nephew, and how happy the family and the neighbors are, and how they circumcised the baby, and about Hebrew naming conventions, and about how Uncle Zechariah is suddenly able to speak again. Luke recites the lyrics to a freestyle rap that Uncle Zechariah performs. He then tells us who is the Roman Emperor at the time and who is the governor of Syria and how they decided to take a census. He tells us about travelling to other towns because you had to be in the correct town to fill out your paperwork. He tells about how Joseph had to fill out the paperwork for himself and his new wife and he tells us that the baby is born.

Wait, what? When was the baby conceived? Mary is a virgin one second, and delivers the baby in the next scene. Didn't Gabriel promise her that something wonderful was going to happen? The Holy Spirit was supposed to come upon her. The power of the Most High was supposed to overshadow her. Did Mary somehow not

---

[274] Luke 1:35

notice this happening? Or did she forget to tell Luke about it in her interview, and he never bothered to ask? Doesn't it seem like kind of an important detail? Or was there foul play involved? Did someone edit Luke's story after the fact? How do we know we got the full version? Something is clearly missing. Why?

Beware Barren Women Bearing Babies

Luke tells us another fact about Mary's cousin Elizabeth and her husband Zechariah. *They were childless because Elizabeth was not able to conceive, and they were both very old.*[275] Elizabeth was "very old" and had never been able to conceive. Yet, after a visit from Gabriel, she bears a son, later to become known as John The Baptist.

So too with Sarah, the wife of Abraham. She was unable to conceive[276] and had long given up hope of ever doing so, so much so that she insisted that Abraham sleep with her handmaid[277], in order to produce an heir. Yet again, after a visit from a heavenly messenger, she does become pregnant after all, bearing Abraham his promised son Isaac. In a twenty-five year period, covered by Genesis chapters 12 to 21, Abraham and his family are visited no less than six times by some kind of extraterrestrial being. Abraham once again experiences the "debar Yahweh"[278], this time accompanied by a floating metallic "smoking firepot with a blazing torch", that flies through their camp.[279] Some years later, Yahweh himself appears to Abraham. "Hang out with me, and become without defect,"

---

[275] Luke 1:7
[276] Genesis 11:30
[277] Genesis 16:2
[278] see page 37
[279] Genesis 15

Yahweh tells Abraham.[280] He uses the same word 'tamim' that he used with Noah. Is he talking about some kind of biological or genetic correction? Less than a year later, Abraham's son is born. Did Yahweh inject Abraham with some kind of super potency hormones? Or did he heal him of some preexisting condition that interfered with his ability to impregnate Sarah?

This same plotline is mirrored once again in the book of Judges. *A certain man of Zorah, named Manoah, from the clan of the Danites, had a wife who was childless, unable to give birth. A messenger from Yahweh appeared to her and said, "You are barren and childless, but you are going to become pregnant and give birth to a son.*[281]

She recounts her encounter to her husband, describing the visitor as an "other of elohim"[282] and "very awesome" and essentially "not from around here". The visitor returns the following day or shortly thereafter. When asked his name, he replies that it is beyond understanding. Then, as they are sitting around the fire-pit, the visitor rose up into the sky[283] In due time, our unnamed heroine gave birth to a son, who they name Samson. Samson became a hero of old in his own right, assisted by the 'ruach elohim',[284] touted as a berserker in battle and reputed to be the world's strongest man. What exactly was in his DNA?

---

[280] Genesis 17:1

[281] Judges 13:2-3

[282] אִישׁ הָאֱלֹהִים (ish ha elohim); the same word (ish) is used for Noah

[283] Judges 13:20

[284] Judges 14:6

Jesus

We may never know exactly how Mary became pregnant, but we certainly do know who her baby would become. Her child Jesus would become quite possibly the most famous man of all time. His birth, life, and death are marked with many strange encounters, including several flying objects whose identity we cannot be entirely sure of. On the evening of Jesus' birth an army of bright flying objects appeared publicly in the countryside near Bethlehem. *There were shepherds living out in the fields nearby, keeping watch over their flocks at night. An angel of the Lord appeared to them, and the glory of the Lord shone around them, and they were terrified. [...] Suddenly a great company of the heavenly host appeared*[285] The objects were then seen flying back up into the sky.

At Jesus' baptism another mysterious aerial phenomenon occurs. According to Luke, *heaven was opened and the Holy Spirit descended on him in bodily form like a dove. And a voice came from heaven: "You are my Son, whom I love; with you I am well pleased."*[286]

Luke makes a point of letting us know that this event was a physical phenomenon, rather than a spiritual, emotional, psychic, or metaphysical occurrence. *In bodily form*, he says, a physical object descended like a dove, and this was preceded by the sky physically opening up. The gospel of Mark concurs, describing this event as "the heavens being torn open".[287] Interestingly, in the following chapter, Luke re-uses this same metaphor about the sky being opened or closed. He says that *in Elijah's time, the sky was shut for three and a half years and there was a*

---

[285] Luke 2:8-15
[286] Luke 3:21-22
[287] Mark 1:10

severe famine throughout the land.[288] There is no doubt that this reference indicates rain, or the lack thereof. This two-sided metaphor clearly associates the sky being shut as the extended absence of rain, and conversely, the sky being opened up as to enable the rain. It is highly likely then that at Jesus' baptism, it began to rain as the sky was opened, just as the strange birdlike object descended from the sky. Luke may be unknowingly providing evidence of a well-known meteorological phenomenon colloquially known as "hole punch clouds" or "fallstreak holes". Numerous studies have shown that due to differences in temperature and air pressure, aircraft passing through cloud layers can trigger the rapid formation of ice crystals, which fall to Earth in a short burst of precipitation, typically melting back into liquid form as rain, and leaving behind a distinctive circular void in the blanket of clouds. This is quite possibly what Luke was referring to as "the heavens opening". If so, this is pretty strong evidence to support Luke's claim of a physical UFO. It is also instructive to note that the same verbiage was used by Ezekiel in describing his own UFO encounter,[289] as well as being explicitly described by David in the Psalms.[290]

After his baptism, Jesus began a public ministry as an itinerant healer. He was not a preacher or prophet. Although he did occasionally engage in public speaking events, his healings outnumber his preaching by perhaps a thousand to one. He had little concern for kings or leaders unless they specifically approached them. He would rather avoid the question than answer someone directly as a prophet would. No, by all accounts his focus was almost purely on healing. And he got results. He was said to have

---

[288] Luke 4:25 referring to 1 Kings 17:1
[289] see page 19
[290] see page 66

healed entire villages or counties, so that not one sick person remained.

How was Jesus able to heal with such consistent and powerful results? Could his techniques be related to those used by Moses? What techniques would those be, you may ask, and rightly so, for we have not yet examined them. We have only covered the circumstances leading up to this rather unique act of Moses. We examined the seraphim that "bit" the Israelites, making many of them very sick, and killing many besides.[291] We noted the connection between the supposed snakebites, and the otherworldly entity that appeared to the prophet Isaiah. They have the same name — "seraphim".

This brings us back to Moses. Moses asked Yahweh for help, possibly using the Ark of the Covenant to communicate. Yahweh told Moses to build a new gadget. Unlike the tabernacle gear, not a lot of detail is given. It seems to resemble the shape of a snake or dragon made of bronze or copper twisted around the top of a pole. Traditionally, this device has become known as the "bronze serpent". But what *is* it? Could it be some kind of antenna? Who knows? We are told that whoever looked at the device was cured of their sickness.[292] The Bible does not indicate what principles were utilized by this device, but it does appear to be a technological artifact. That is to say, there are no magic ceremonies, potions, incantations, or offerings called for. After being assembled, the device just works. We just don't know how. Could it be that Jesus' healing was similar? Did Jesus use some kind of unknown technology to heal? We may never know. However, Jesus does draw our attention to this matter in a very direct manner, should one have eyes to see the connection. In Matthew chapter 13, Jesus speaks of *the knowledge of the*

---

[291] see page 98
[292] Numbers 21:8-9

mysteries of the kingdom of heaven[293] then immediately quotes the prophet Isaiah, using the core statement from Isaiah's own UFO encounter. *They might see with their eyes, hear with their ears, understand with their hearts, and turn **and be healed.***[294]

Who was it that told Isaiah this message in the first place? None other than the seraphim.[295] The seraphim explicitly tells Isaiah that this knowledge will be understood by very few, but that it contains healing power for those open-minded enough to embrace it. Jesus then chooses this exact statement to explain his own healing practices. It seems as though Jesus based his entire ministry around some kind of hidden knowledge or alien technology that enabled him to heal people.

A variety of information-based healing approaches have been developed and utilized with efficacy within the modern psychotherapy profession. Notably, Neuro-linguistic programming (NLP), and Eye Movement Desensitization and Reprocessing (EMDR), are two which have gained considerable popularity. Though these two approaches differ greatly, they both have in common the fact that they are essentially allowing the patient to alter thought patterns and improve certain aspects of their mental state by basically (to put it simply) reprogramming their brain. Jesus himself stated this concept explicitly, saying: *You will know the truth and the truth shall set you free*[296]

Jesus offered another important conceptual clue. He spoke often in a metaphor of *light*. He spoke of light banishing darkness. In this way the concept is similar to knowledge, for where knowledge goes, the world is changed and enlightened. There is no doubt that knowledge

---

[293] Matthew 13:11
[294] Matthew 13:15, Isaiah 6:10
[295] Isaiah 6:1-10
[296] John 8:32

was a component of Jesus' paradigm; *"hold to my teaching"*[297] he told his disciples. What is teaching but the passing on of knowledge? More enigmatically he said to them *"I am the light of the world. Whoever follows me will never walk in darkness, but will have the light of life."*[298]

Jesus also drew a fascinating technological connection between himself and many of the mysterious alien technologies that have been discussed in this book. Jesus claims some kind parallel between himself, Yahweh, Moses' "bronze serpent", and the UFO encountered by Isaiah.

Jesus said, "When you have lifted up the Son of Man, then you will know that I am he and that I do nothing on my own but speak just what the Father has taught me. The one who sent me is with me; he has not left me alone.[299]

The sheer complexity of layering in this short verse is stunning. Biblical scholars concur that the phrase "lifted up" refers undoubtedly back to the "bronze serpent", as well as being a foreshadowing of his own death by crucifixion. Even the crown of thorns[300] which he will be forced to wear, figures back to the twisted copper serpentine form mounted atop the pole.[301]

This brings us to a little bit of physics. By definition, any twisted coil of metal creates a simple electronic component known as an inductor, or coil. If the coil is unshielded,[302] it will also act as an antenna with a specific resonant frequency. It will respond to a certain frequency of electromagnetic waves. Whether Yahweh and Moses intended to or not, they built a rudimentary radio

---

[297] John 8:31
[298] John 8:12
[299] John 8:28-29
[300] Matthew 27:29
[301] Numbers 21:8
[302] see page 103

receiver.[303] Since Moses was told to hold the staff in the air we can deduce that it was not touching the ground, and since it seems to have lacked any wiring specifically going to the ground, this contraption would have not only been unshielded and ungrounded, but Moses' raising it into the air would have made if a very effective antenna. This does not in any way imply the existence of a radio transmitter to go with it. The circuitry may well have been reading dead air. But then, why build it?

The electromagnetic spectrum is an essentially limitless band of numbers. Some of these numbers correspond to what we typically would call radio waves. Other numbers correspond to what we recognize as light. These waves exist in nature. Sunlight is actually electromagnetic waves. The critical point is that these different terminologies are misleading. Light and radio waves are simply larger or smaller numbers. There is no fundamental difference between them in terms of physics. We only think of them differently because we have developed different technologies focusing on different number ranges. The physiology of the human eye allows us to see only a certain small range of this spectrum. We think of that as light. But we are thinking of it wrong.

---

[303] I want to be very clear that I am not implying the existence of any particular modulation or encoding protocols, which are necessary to turn the reception of a radio wave into the reception of a "signal" or "message". The bronze serpent does not appear to include a demodulator, so we can be relatively certain that it could not interpret AM or FM radio protocols as we know them. It also did not include a tunable component, so it would have acted as a simple resonant circuit. This does not inhibit its usefulness though, since if Yahweh had been intending to use it as a receiver, he could have designed the transmitter on his end to be tuned to match the existing receiver circuitry. Even so, this very basic setup would allow the sending and receiving of a simple single frequency electromagnetic wave.

When Jesus speaks of light, he may very well be thinking beyond these artificially constructed limits. Is it possible that Jesus somehow knew that all objects, including human bodies, constantly both emit and absorb electromagnetic radiation? Jesus here refers to himself as the "son of man"[304] which is a rather strange nickname if you think about it. It might be a reference to one of several passages in the Book of Enoch, which Jesus had probably studied, but which is beyond the scope of this book. Jesus then makes a bold statement — *I am he.*[305] The "he" here refers to "the father", or in other words, Yahweh. Jesus says he is Yahweh. In fact, this is a recursive definition, because Yahweh, in Hebrew is יְהֹוָה, which is derived from אֶהְיֶה which literally means "I am", and is the spelling used by Yahweh upon first revealing himself to Moses at the "burning bush" encounter.[306] Yahweh answers Moses' question "what is your name" with "I am 'I AM'". So, when Jesus equates himself with Yahweh he is effectively saying "I am 'I am *I AM*'". It is perhaps a statement that only a mathematician can love. Nevertheless, Jesus continues; *"I do nothing on my own but speak just what the Father has taught me."*[307] This statement again is reminiscent of the concept of the radio antenna. A radio only repeats what it hears. Jesus claims to be merely a channel. And not only that, but he says that the radio is always on; *"The one who sent me is with me; he has not left me alone."*[308]

Is it possible then, that Jesus, knowing his human body was constantly absorbing electromagnetic radiation across a wide band of both visible light and invisible wavelengths, somehow was able to "tune into" and decode

---

[304] John 8:28
[305] Ibid.
[306] Exodus 3:14
[307] John 8:28
[308] John 8:29

some kind of secret signals using nothing more than his own body and some hidden knowledge of protocols? This seems very far-fetched, until one considers that Jesus did explicitly state that he was privy to some kind of hidden knowledge — *the knowledge of the mysteries of the kingdom of heaven.*[309] But if that were the case, how did he come about such knowledge? If he somehow had tapped into a hidden "radio station", he might have learned secret information through that channel. But this doesn't solve the problem, because where did he learn how to use the secret radio in the first place? Perhaps, rather than how, this is really a question of where. And if so, Jesus provides the answer.

Jesus claimed to be from another world. In fact, he made a lengthy series of wild statements relating to this claim. Let us examine these, in his own words:

- I am not from this world - John 8:23
- I am from above - John 8:23
- Before Abraham was born, I am! - John 8:58
- I am telling you what I have seen in the Father's presence - John 8:38
- I have come here from God. I have not come on my own; God sent me - John 8:42
- I am going away; where I go, you cannot come. - John 8:21
- you have no idea where I come from or where I am going - John 8:14
- Whoever belongs to God hears what God says. The reason you do not hear is that you do not belong to God. - John 8:47

---

[309] Matthew 13:11

Jesus essentially admitted that he is from another planet (in space, not another dimension) and he is very old; he is the one they call Yahweh, and he works for the Elohim, who sent him to earth, and to whom he will return upon completing his mission.

That's a lot of information to digest. Given Jesus' key position at the heart of our well-known and cherished religion, this suggestion requires a radical paradigm shift. Many readers may find welling up within them a desire to burn this book. It would be completely understandable if they chose to do so. The people of Jesus day reacted the same way: *At this, they picked up stones to stone him, but Jesus hid himself, slipping away from the temple grounds.*[310] But Jesus promised to *send the Spirit of truth. The world cannot accept him, because it neither sees him nor knows him.*[311]

The truth that Jesus spoke plainly of was not hidden in parables. It was not some fairy tale. He did not speak of inaccessible dimensions in some far future eschatology requiring atonement. The kingdom of heaven was and is at hand for those who simply believe his acts and his words. This was always Jesus' message. This is Jesus' only message. Jesus understood that this paradigm is largely incompatible with normal life. It is a world-shaking revelation. It is difficult to accept. And that's alright. One can take the information and do with it what they must. There is no judgement. No punishment. No guilt. Here's the story. It is what it is. Accept it, or don't.

Jesus did, however, slip away. Rather than stand there waiting for the crowd to stone him, he "hid himself". Was this accomplished through some other kind of light manipulation? Jesus *was* the light. Light can be absorbed as well as reflected. Light can be amplified or nullified. Light

---

[310] John 8:59
[311] John 14:17

can be seen or unseen. Light can be familiar, or unknown. Jesus was anything but familiar.

Jesus took with him Peter, James and John the brother of James, and led them up a high mountain by themselves. There he was transfigured before them. His face shone like the sun, and his clothes became as white as the light. Just then there appeared before them Moses and Elijah, talking with Jesus.[312]

Like Moses on Mt. Sinai, the men ascend a mountain.[313] Like the apostle Paul, there is a light as bright as the sun. But unlike previous encounters, two historical figures miraculously emerge — none other than Moses and Elijah.

It might not be surprising to see Elijah here. After all, he was taken up into the sky and was reported to have escaped death. Moses, though, was dead. How is it possible that he showed up over a thousand years later, alive? And for that matter, how is it possible that the disciples recognized these two figures? It's not as if they had seen photographs of them, had they? Then again, according to the text, Moses and Elijah talked with Jesus, so it is entirely conceivable that Peter James and John heard their conversation and were able to identify them either contextually, or from Moses and Elijah literally using their names to address each other or identify themselves to Jesus.

Another possibility is that the disciples misidentified one of the men. According to a few extra details given by our consummate journalist, Luke, the disciples were "very sleepy"[314], a common effect reported by modern UFO witnesses, and especially abductees. In their groggy state, some details may have been foggy. Rather than Elijah and Moses, is it possible that the two

---

[312] Matthew 17:1-3
[313] possibly even the same mountain, Mt. Sinai
[314] Luke 9:32

men may have Elijah and Enoch? Both Elijah and Enoch were still alive, as far we know, since they were both taken aboard UFOs and never reported as having died. Luke 16:26 is clear that the dead cannot return to the living, so the Enoch explanation is the only option which fits with that particular Christian doctrine. Another optional way out of this conundrum would be that it was truly Moses as Peter James and John state. Perhaps Moses had been aboard the ship all along and had not died either. Of course, this interpretation raises issues with the biblical account of Moses' death and burial.[315]

Luke gleans one additional bit of information from his research. Whoever they really were, the two historical figures spoke to Jesus of his upcoming departure,[316] an event which Jesus was apparently planning with whoever was in charge of UFO scheduling. Luke brings our attention to this fact again a few verses later — *As the **time approached** for him to be **taken up to heaven**, Jesus resolutely set out for Jerusalem.*[317] It seems that Elijah and the other man (who may or may not have been Enoch[318]) came to talk to Jesus in order to arrange the final details of where and when they would return to pick him up. At any rate, the next thing they knew, *a bright cloud covered them, and a voice from the cloud said, "This is my Son, whom I love; with him I am well pleased. Listen to him!"*[319] This verse combines elements from Jesus' baptism, with the classic Mosaic element of the descending clouds. When the

---

[315] Deuteronomy 34:5-7

[316] Luke 9:31

[317] Luke 9:51

[318] This supposition is further supported by an apocryphal tale where Noah's father Lamech goes to visit Enoch (after he was taken), then returns to his family. Again, this shows that Enoch was somewhere accessible but not on earth.

[319] Matthew 17:5

men looked up after a moment of fear, Moses and Elijah had disappeared once again, along with the shining cloud.

From shining clouds, we turn to dark clouds, for the next event with possible UFO involvement is a dark day known as the Crucifixion. Matthew states that *from noon until three in the afternoon darkness came over all the land.*[320] Although clouds and even dark thick clouds have been associated with many of the encounters examined previously, one would be hard pressed to correlate clouds dark enough to be described as Matthew puts it. Unless, that is, one were to factor in the words of David in the Psalms and John in Revelation. If the entire fleet of "thousands of thousands"[321] of flying machines were to suddenly appear, especially considering the accompanying effects of smoke and fire with which they are typically seen, and the possibility of weather disturbances caused by these metallic objects, then perhaps such darkness could indeed be accounted for. How many UFOs would it take to blot out the sun even without clouds? A million might just do it. If we are to take David seriously, we have to realize that when he says, "thousands of thousands" he is literally saying "millions".

Jesus' resurrection was witnessed only after the event itself. His empty grave was found in the morning, but nobody was hanging around his grave at night to tell us if they saw anything unusual in the sky that night. At least that's what the Gospel of Mark would have us believe. Matthew, however, recounts a shining object descending from the sky, witnessed by several roman guards, and attested to by Mary Magdalene and "the other Mary", who spoke to the shining extraterrestrial.

There was a violent earthquake, for an angel of the Lord came down from heaven and, going to the tomb, rolled

---

[320] Matthew 27:45

[321] Psalm 68:17

back the stone and sat on it. His appearance was like lightning, and his clothes were white as snow.[322]

That evening Jesus told his friends more about his upcoming plan: *"I am going to send you what my Father has promised; but stay in the city until you have been clothed with power from on high."*[323] Then they all went for a midnight walk, and *when he had led them out to the vicinity of Bethany, he lifted up his hands and blessed them. While he was blessing them, he left them and was taken up into heaven.*[324]

Jesus' mission here was accomplished. The appointed time had come. Jesus walked to the agreed upon location and ascended in the same manner as Elijah and Enoch.

---

[322] Matthew 28:2-3
[323] Luke 24:49
[324] Luke 24:50-51

The 5th Kind - Inviting Contact

As various bible characters have demonstrated, close encounters may be mystifying, stunning, dazzling, or frightening. Many people may consider such an encounter the stuff of nightmares. But a growing number of people find the idea of such an experience desirable and possibly even intentionally attainable. Dr Steven Greer has developed what he has termed "CE-5 Protocols", specifically designed to help people achieve their goals of a UFO encounter, by purposefully initiating contact. The purposeful initiation of contact is the defining feature of "close encounters of the fifth kind." This desire is not new. The prophet Isaiah, after having experienced the UFO phenomenon once, yearned for another such experience. He wrote longingly:

Oh, that you would rend the heavens and come down, that the mountains would tremble before you! As when fire sets twigs ablaze and causes water to boil, come down to make your name known to your enemies and cause the nations to quake before you! For when you did awesome things that we did not expect, you came down, and the mountains trembled before you.[325]

Although Isaiah's longing may have been unrequited, it has been demonstrated that David was able to successfully cause Yahweh to appear. He tells us as much in one of his songs:

---

[325] Isaiah 64:1-3

> *"In my distress I called to the Lord;*
> *I called out to my God.*
> *From his temple he heard my voice;*
> *my cry came to his ears. [...]*
> *He parted the heavens and came down;*
> *dark clouds were under his feet.*
> *He mounted the cherubim and flew;*[326]

David was able to call upon Yahweh, apparently using only his voice. Yahweh responded with metallic ships that "opened the sky".[327] Many times David sought advice "from upstairs". The phrase *"David inquired of the Lord"* is often repeated in the scriptures[328], usually with dramatic and strategic effect.[329] There is reason to believe that David may have used the Ark of the Covenant or possibly the Urim and Thummim for such inquiries[330], although this is not explicitly indicated in most instances. Often, the impression one gets from the reading is that David simply prayed. The simple act of asking can be effective, as evidenced by the example of Rebekah, who lived several hundred years before the Ark of the Covenant even existed.

Rebekah became pregnant. The babies jostled each other within her, and she said, "Why is this happening to me?" So she went to inquire of Yahweh. Yahweh said to

---

[326] Psalm 18:6, 9-10

[327] see page 165

[328] 1 Samuel 23:1, Joshua 15:21, 1 Samuel 30:8, 2 Samuel 2:1, 2 Samuel 5:19, 2 Samuel 5:23, 2 Samuel 21:1

[329] 2 Samuel 5:24 As soon as you hear the sound of marching in the tops of the poplar trees, move quickly, because that will mean the Lord has gone out in front of you to strike the Philistine army.

[330] 1 Samuel 28:6 refers explicitly to the Urim and Thummim, stating that Saul tried unsuccessfully to inquire with them.

her, *"Two nations are in your womb, and two peoples from within you will be separated*[331]

It seems that Rebekah *went* somewhere to perform her inquiry but did not appear to have to use any special tools or routines. The requirement of a certain location in order to perform inquiries to Yahweh seems to be supported throughout scripture. When the kings of Judah and Israel were conferring regarding ongoing treaties and allegiances, in order to inquire of Yahweh, they had to move their meetings to some surprising locations, such as the *threshing floor by the entrance of the gate of Samaria*,[332] indicating that they definitely took location into account for such inquiries, and not according to normal criteria. They left their palaces and went out to a farm because there was something special about the place.

King Jehoshaphat (king of Judah) said to the king of Israel *inquire today for the debar Yahweh.*[333] As we have previously examined, the debar Yahweh is something more substantial than a voice or a message. It may very well be a UFO. It might even be technologically tied to a specific location.

The debar Yahweh came also to Jeremiah, at his behest. The narration makes a point that Jeremiah was free to roam, for he had not yet become a prisoner of war.[334] The point does not seem pertinent to the story other than perhaps to indicate that Jeremiah was able to travel to one of the appropriate predetermined places. Was this because the debar could only be summoned from certain locations? Each time we read about such encounters, they seem to occur at a well-known holy place, or they become known as a holy place after said encounter. The obvious exception

---

[331] Genesis 25:21-23
[332] 1 Kings 22:10
[333] 1 Kings 22:5
[334] Jeremiah 37:3-6

is that of the encounters associated with holy objects, or in other words, portable locations, such as the Tabernacle and the Tent of Meeting. Both of these are clearly associated with descending UFOs, as we have already seen.

Summoning War

Whereas the examples above tended to be fairly instructional or even conversational in nature, we soon find that intentions are not always so peaceful. Often the intentions of the CE-5 initiate were military.

After the death of Saul, his general launched a coup by unauthorizedly installing Saul's son as king over the southern half of the kingdom, setting up his new capital city at a place called *Mahanaim*.[335] This act began a long period of civil war and division within the nation, splitting the country into two, Israel, and Judah. The relevance to this discussion is rather a side topic of the narrative, but it is a distinctly telling one. The city of Mahanaim just so happened to be built on the exact spot upon which Jacob first witnessed the army of the elohim.[336] It had been revered as a special place because of Jacob's encounter. The rebel faction of Saul's followers were hoping for a further encounter, so they went to a place that was known as being a UFO hot-spot, in the hopes that Yahweh would appear with his extraterrestrial advanced weaponry and back their conspiracy.

In Isaiah 37 (and confirmed in 2 Kings 19), Isaiah successfully summoned what he called "the angel of the lord" — most likely the same seraphim who had visited him in Isaiah 6. This seraphim then proceeded to kill the entire Assyrian army of 185,000 soldiers.[337]

---

[335] 2 Samuel 2:8-9
[336] see page 10
[337] Isaiah 37:36

Summoning Peace

Although biblical military incursions were occasionally backed by UFO warships, these violent encounters remain the minority. In general, the typical biblical UFO encounter is not a harmful experience to the witnesses, aside from an understandable initial fear and the long-lasting shock and awe of learning great mysteries.

Enoch, Noah, and Abraham walked with the elohim. They hung out. They conversed. They learned amazing things — many of which they could not share. The writer of the book of Hebrews calls this faith:

By faith Enoch was taken from this life, so that he did not experience death: He could not be found, because God had taken him away. For before he was taken, he was commended as one who pleased God. And without faith it is impossible to please God, because anyone who comes to him must believe that he exists and that he rewards those who earnestly seek him.[338]

The elohim hung out with these men. Ordinary men with two factors in common. They believed that the elohim exist, and they earnestly sought contact. Such contact mirrors the Edenic state of Adam and Eve, the perfect, uncorrupted ideal. They walked with the elohim in the garden. Yahweh pleads for a return to this state of peaceful communication:

If my people, who are called by my name, will humble themselves and pray and seek my face and turn from their wicked ways, then I will hear from heaven[339]

Yahweh has been consistent in his message. Each prophet has received and declared this same message. Is this not the core message of the bible? Is it not the gospel?

---

[338] Hebrews 11:5-6
[339] 2 Chronicles 7:14

Conclusion

Are UFOs real? The question is highly complex, fraught with logical pitfalls, and according to many, lacking in truly concrete evidence. However, if the UFO phenomenon is even slightly real, it must inform our every other notion. History, legend, and religion cannot be thought of as separate from the UFO phenomenon.

As far as the question at hand, *"what does the Bible have to say about UFOs?"* — the answer seems to have become abundantly obvious to anyone who would read it with an open mind and heart. The Bible very clearly and repeatedly describes UFOs and the sane, rational witnesses to them. It does so in a consistent, non-contradictory manner. It does so across history. It does so at the highest levels of government and religion. It does so in a way that is enlightening rather than frightening, hopeful rather than upsetting. It extends a message of welcome and unity, of ancient truths hidden in plain sight for all who have ears to hear.

Appendices

Appendix A: A Chronology of Biblical UFO Encounters

- the Elohim create earth, Gen 1
- Yahweh in Eden, Gen 3
- Nephilim born with Elohim DNA, p 152, Gen 6
- Enoch's abduction, p 144, 173, Gen 5, Heb 11
- Noah, p 153, Gen 6
~ 1550 BC - Abraham's promise, p 45, narrative missing
Abraham and the smoking firepot, Gen 15
~ 1470 - Rebekah's inquiry, p 178, Gen 25
~ 1450 BC - Jacob's ladder, p15, Gen 28
Jacob and the two camps, p 10, Gen 32
Jacob's wrestling match, p 11, Gen 32
~ 1300 BC - Moses and the "burning bush", p 42, Ex 3
Aaron's speech interrupted, p 42, Ex 16
the Sinai encounters, p 41, 54, Ex 19, 24
Bezalel trained, p 71, Ex 31
millions led through the desert, p 7
~ 1260 BC - Joshua's recording stone, p 130, Jsh 24
      death of Nahab and Abihu, p 93, Lev 10
~ 1080 BC - Manoah, p 163, Jdg 13
Samson, p 163, Jdg 14
~1000 BC - David's encounters, p 62, 2 Sam 22, Psa 18
      death of Uzzah, p 93, 2 Sam 6
~860 BC - Jehoshaphat's inquiry, p 179, 1 Ki 22
~ 842 BC - Elijah & the still small voice, p 37, 1 Ki 19
Elijah's abduction, p 145, 2 Ki 2
740 BC - Isaiah's encounter, p87, Isa 6
~ 590 BC - Ezekiel's 1st encounter, p 19, Eze 1
587 BC - Jeremiah calls the debar, p 179, Jer 37

~ 584 BC - Ezekiel's 2nd encounter, p 77, Eze 8-10
537 BC - Daniel and the emerald man, p 47, Dan 10
522 BC - Daniel and Gabriel, p 51, Dan 9
520 BC - Zechariah's first encounter, p 40, Zech 1
520 BC - Zechariah & the "bird women", p 40, Zech 1
~ 4 BC - Zechariah (priest) dumbstruck, p 160, Luke 1
Elizabeth's visitation, p 162, Luke 1
Mary's visitations, p 159, Matt 1
The Bethlehem encounters, p 5, Matt 2
~ 30 CE - Jesus' ministry
    the two Marys, p 175, Matt 28
~ 35 CE - Philip's transportation, p 148, Acts 8
Paul, p 149, 2 Cor 12, Acts 9
~ 90 CE - John's revelation, p 141, Rev 1, 4, 21

Appendix B: Index of Bible Characters

(in order of appearance in this book)

The three wise men, p 5, Matthew 2
Moses, p 7, 41, 172, Exodus 13, Matthew 17
Jacob, p 10, 11
The elohim, p 19, 11-13, Gen 32, Gen 1
Ezekiel, p 18, 77, 147, Ezekiel 1, 8
Elijah, p 37, 120, 145, 172, 1 Kings 19, 2 Kings 2, Matthew 17
Zechariah (the prophet), p 39, Zechariah 1
Aaron, p 42, 109, Exodus 16, 24
Abraham, p 45, 162, Genesis 12, 22
Daniel, p 47, Daniel 10
Gabriel, p 51, 160, Daniel 9, Luke 1
David, p 62, 140, 178, Psalm 18, 2 Sam 22
Bezalel, p 71, Exodus 31
Isaiah, p 84, 87, Isaiah 6, 37
Nahab and Abihu, p 93, Leviticus 10
Uzzah, p 93, 2 Sam 6
Joshua, p 100, 116, Exodus 33:11, Joshua 3
John, p 141, Revelation 1, 4, 21
Enoch, p 144, 173, Genesis 5, Hebrews 11
Philip, p 148, Acts 8
Paul, p 149, 2 Corinthians 12, Acts 9
Noah, p 153, Genesis 6
Mary, p 159, Matthew 1
Luke, p 160, Luke 1
Zechariah (the priest), p 160, Luke 1
Elizabeth, p 162, Luke 1
Manoah, p 163, Judges 13
Samson, p 163, Judges 14
Jesus, p 163, Luke 3, Mark 1
the shepherds, p 164, Luke 2
the two Marys, p 175, Matthew 28

Rebekah, p 178, Genesis 25
Jeremiah, p 179, Jeremiah 37
Jehoshaphat, p 179, 1 Kings 22

Appendix C: Index of Hebrew Words

(in order of appearance in this book)

מַלְאֲכֵי אֱלֹהִים: (malake elohim) 'messengers from the gods', p 10

מַחֲנֵה אֱלֹהִים: (mahaneh elohim) 'camp of the gods', p 11

אִישׁ (ish) 'other, alien', p 12, Gen 32

אֲנָשִׁים (anasim) 'human', p 12, Gen 32

סֻלָּם (sulam) מֻצָּב (mussab) אַרְצָה (arsah) וְרֹאשׁוֹ (werosow) מַגִּיעַ (maggia) הַשָּׁמָיְמָה (hassamayema)
"he saw a strange object land on the ground whose head arrived from the sky." p 15-16, Gen 28

עֹלִים (olim) 'went up', p 17, Gen 28

וְיֹרְדִים בּוֹ: (weyoredim bo) unknown meaning, p 17, Gen 28

עָלָיו (alaw) unclear meaning, p 17m Gen 28

אוֹפַן (owpan) 'spinning object', p 22, Ezek 1

בָּאָרֶץ (ba-ares) 'on earth', p 23, Ezek 1

וּמַעֲשֵׂיהֶם (uma-asehem) 'machinery', p 24, Ezek 1

בְּתוֹךְ (betowk) 'within', p 25, Ezek 1

וְגַבֵּיהֶן (wegabbehen) 'armour', p 26, Ezek 1

וְיִרְאָה (weyirah) 'fearsome', p 26, Ezek 1

עֵינַיִם (enayim) 'eyes, metaphorically lights, p 26, Ezek 1

דְּמוּת (demut) 'image', p 27, Ezek 1

מַרְאֵיהֶן (marahen) 'resemblance', p 27, Ezek 1

פָּנִים (panim) 'edge', p 28, Ezek 1

כְּנָפַיִם (kenapayim) 'edge/wing', p 29, Ezek 1

וִידֵי (wi-de) 'hands, craftsmanship', p 29, Ezek 1

מִתַּחַת (mittahat) 'under', p 30, Ezek 1

וּדְמוּת, (udemut) possible reference to the Babylonian Lamassu, p 30, Ezek 1

סַפִּיר (sappir) 'sapphire', p 32, Ezek 1

אָדָם (adam) 'human', p 33, Ezek 1

דְּבַר־יְהוָה (debar Yahweh) 'command/action', p 37, 1 Kings 19, Judges 19, Deut 22

קוֹל (qowl) 'voice', p 39, 1 Kings 19

כְּבוֹד (kevod) 'chariot', p 41, Exodus 16
הַסְּנֶה (hasseneh) unknown meaning but not 'bush', p 43, 54, Exodus 3, Deuteronomy 33
בַּסְּבַךְ (bassebak) 'bush', p 43, Genesis 22, Isaiah 9, 10, Psalm 74
שִׂיחַ (siah) 'bushes', p 43, Genesis 2, 21, Job 30
אֶחָד (ehad) 'one', p 48, Daniel 10
אִישׁ (ish) 'male', p 48, Daniel 10, Genesis 7
בַּדִּים (baddim) 'specialized fabric', p 48, Daniel 10
כְּתַרְשִׁישׁ (ketarsis) 'emerald', p 48, Daniel 10
וּפָנָיו (upanaw) 'in front of', p 49, Daniel 10
וְעֵינָיו (wa-enaw) 'eyes/vision', p 49, Daniel 10
וַיִּרְאוּ (wayyiru) 'stunning realization', p 58, Exodus 24
וְתַחַת (wetahat) 'instead', p 59, Exodus 24
רַגְלָיו (raglaw) 'enduring base', p 59, Exodus 24
כְּמַעֲשֵׂה (kema-aseh) 'machine', p59, Exodus 24
לִבְנַת (libnat) 'softwood', p 60, Exodus 24
וּכְעֶצֶם (uke-esem) 'structure/(bones)', p 60, Exodus 24
הַשָּׁמַיִם (hassamayim) 'space', p 60, Exodus 24
לָטֹהַר (latohar) 'clarity', p60, Exodus 24
וּבַנְּחֹשֶׁת (ubannehoset) 'copper', p 72, Exodus 31
כִּלְאַיִם (kilayim) 'diverse kinds', p 73, Leviticus 19
לַחְשֹׁב (lahsob) 'calculate/design', p 73, Exodus 31
מַחֲשָׁבֹת (mahasabot) 'plans/purposes', p 74, Exodus 31
לַעֲשׂוֹת (la-asowet) 'active', p 74, Exodus 31
וָאֲמַלֵּא (wa-amal-le) 'full', p 75, Exodus 31
רוּחַ (ruach) 'spirit/style/technology', p75, Exodus 31
הַגַּלְגַּל (haggalgal) jargon for the 'wheels', p 81, Ezekiel 10
כַּפֹּרֶת (kapporet) jargon for the 'covering', p 85, Exodus 25
שְׂרָפִים (seraphim) 'six winged burning snakes', p 87, Isaiah 6, 14, Numbers 21, Deut 8
סֹכְכִים (sokekim) 'guardians', p 87, Exodus 37
הַצִּרְעָה (hassirah) 'hornet', p 95, Exodus 23
צָרַעַת (saraat) 'leprosy', p 95, Leviticus 13
הַנְּחָשִׁים (hannehasim), 'snake/serpent', p 98, Numbers 21
וַיְנַשְּׁכוּ (way-nas-seku) 'bite', p 98, Numbers 21

זֵר (zer) 'connector', p 102, Exodus 25
קַרְסֵי (qarsei) 'clasps', p 102, Exodus 26, 36
לֻלָאֹת (lulaot) 'loops', p 102, Exodus 26, 36
עֲשֵׂה־ (aseh) 'enact', p 112, Exodus 32
יֵלְכוּ (yeleku) 'travel', p 112, Exodus 32
לְפָנֵינוּ (lepanenu) 'before', p 112, Exodus 32
מַסֵּכָה (mas-se-kah) unclear meaning, p114, Exodus 32
כְּכַלֹּתוֹ (kekalotow) 'it came to pass', p 124, Exodus 31
וַיִּתֵּן (wayitin) 'was given', p 124, Exodus 31
לְדַבֵּר (ledab-ber) 'meeting', p 124, Exodus 31
כְּתֻבִים (ketubim) 'recorded', p 124, Exodus 31
פֶּסֶל־ (pesel) 'cut', p129, Exodus 34
בַּהֲעָלוֹת (beha-alo-wt) 'offer', p 146, 2 Kings 2
בַּסְעָרָה (basarah) 'a storm', p 146, 2 Kings 2
הַשָּׁמַיִם (hassamayim) 'space-men', p 146, 2 Kings 2
תַּבְנִית (tabnit) 'of similar function', p 147, Ezekiel 8
יָד (yad) 'hand/(figuratively) power', p 147, Ezekiel 8
הִתְהַלֶּךְ (hit-hal-lek) 'hang out', p 153, Genesis 6
אֵלֶּה (eleh) 'these', p 154, Genesis 6
תּוֹלְדֹת (toldot) 'ancestry', p 154, Genesis 6
אִישׁ (ish) 'other', p 155, Genesis 6
צַדִּיק (saddiq) 'righteous', p 155, Genesis 6
תָּמִים (tamim) 'free of defect', p 155, Genesis 6
הָיָה (hayah) 'had become', p 155, Genesis 6
בְּדֹרֹתָיו (bedorotaw) 'future generations', p 155, Genesis 6
אֶהְיֶה (Yahweh) 'I am', p 170, Exodus 3, John 8

Appendix D: Ancient Hebrew, Dead Languages, and Hapax Legomena

Hapax legomenon (plural: hapax legomena) is a Greek phrase used in biblical exegesis to indicate a certain class of words that are difficult or impossible to translate. The literal meaning is "said only once". In the strictest sense, it refers to a word that appears uniquely in one place in the Old or New Testament. A slightly expanded definition includes words which are used multiple times, but in a very limited context, lacking comparators in "normal" literary use.

Hapax legomena are particularly critical in the Old Testament, due to several simple historical facts. Unlike the ancient Greek of the New Testament, where countless cultural exemplars abound for lexical comparison, the ancient Hebrew of the Old Testament lacks a comparable body of literature. The ancient Hebrews did not adopt the practice of inscribing clay tablets like early Mesopotamian cultures. Nor did they erect massive stone monuments covered with inscriptions. Instead, they were accustomed to the more advanced technologies of Egypt; specifically, writing with ink on papyrus or parchment. This allowed greater flexibility for a nomadic nation with restrictive storage and portage limitations.

Problems arose, however, in times of war. Whenever Israel was invaded, sacked, pillaged, and carried into captivity, their holy texts were in grave danger of destruction. Layered on top of this is the frequent wavering of Israel between internal and external religious policies and beliefs over hundreds of years. These factors appear to have allowed for the possible loss of continuity of the Hebrew written record, and the certain loss of oral and cultural subtleties and specialties which affect hapax legomena.

Even if the written records were never entirely lost or forgotten (a question of which there is some debate, but which scripture itself seems to support[340]) the Hebrew language experienced the natural evolution and attrition that all languages do over time, and was under heavy influence from adjacent language groups for extended periods and from literal occupation, annexation, and colonization from global superpowers, eventually resulting in Hebrew becoming, for all intents and purposes, a dead language.

The Hebrew scriptures thus are forced to act as their own "Rosetta stone". Our modern understanding of Hebrew is based entirely on these texts. This is why the context of usage of any given word is so influential. This is also why, effectively, when a word appears a dozen times, but always in reference to the same specific object, there really is only a single occurrence from a contextual point of view, and therefore any meaning we attribute to that word is decidedly arbitrary, even if guided by educated guesses and best intentions.

---

[340] 2 Kings 22

About the Author

Ken Goudsward is a best-selling author and independent researcher whose interests include archaeology, ontography, epistemology, thaumaturgy, and hermeneutics. He writes in a variety of genres, including non-fiction, science fiction, dark comedy, and poetry.

https://dimensionfold.com/authors/ken-goudsward/

Further Resources

Additional related material, updates extrapolations, extensions, etc. will be available at:

https://ufo.dimensionfold.com/

www.ingramcontent.com/pod-product-compliance
Lightning Source LLC
Chambersburg PA
CBHW071432070526
44578CB00001B/85